Training the Mind in the Great Way

D1041837

Training the Mind in the Great Way

by Gyalwa Gendun Druppa,
the First Dalai Lama (1391-1474)

Foreword by H. H. the Dalai Lama
Translated by Glenn H. Mullin

Snow Lion Publications
Ithaca, New York

Snow Lion Publications
P.O. Box 6483
Ithaca, New York 14851
USA

Copyright © 1993 Glenn H. Mullin

Drawings of Atisha and the First Dalai Lama by Robert Beer

All rights reserved. No part of this book may be reproduced by
any means without prior written permission from the publisher.

Printed in the USA

ISBN 0-937938-96-3

Library of Congress Cataloging-in-Publication Data

Dge-'dun-grub, Dalai Lama I, 1391-1474.
    [Theg pa chen po'i blo sbyoṅ gi gdams pa. English]
    Training the mind in the great way / by Gyalwa Gendun Druppa, the
First Dalai Lama (1391-1474) ; translated by Glenn H. Mullin.
      p. cm.
    Translation of: Theg pa chen po'i blo sbyoṅ gi gdams pa.
    Includes bibliographical references.
    ISBN 0-937938-96-3
    1. Spiritual life (Buddhism)—Early works to 1800.   2. Dge-lugs-pa
(Sect)—Doctrines—Early works to 1800.   3. Atīśa, 982-1054.
    I. Mullin, Glenn H.   II. Title.
BQ7935.D494T4813   1991
294.3'444—dc20
                                   91-26353
                                       CIP

Contents

THE DALAI LAMA

FOREWORD

The tradition of *Lojong Dondunma*, or *Seven Points for Training the Mind*, is an oral transmission of meditative techniques for spiritual development that comes down to us in a line of transmission deriving from the Indonesian Buddhist master Serlingpa, who lived in the late tenth and early eleventh centuries. Serlingpa studied in India for many years, and then returned to his homeland of Shri Vijaya. Numerous lineages from him were brought to Tibet by the venerable Atisha Dipamkara, who had travelled to Indonesia from India and trained there for twelve years. Atisha later was invited to the Land of Snows, and taught the Tibetans until his death. It is said that although he had studied with many different teachers, his Indonesian guru Serlingpa remained most close to his heart, and that tears would come to his eyes whenever he even mentioned this master's name.

Atisha transmitted numerous lineages of instruction in Tibet. These were passed down first to his disciple Lama Drom, and then to Lama Drom's three chief disciples known as 'the Three Kadampa Brothers.' They in turn passed the lineages to their disciples, and so on over the generations. In this way Serlingpa's teachings have come down to us today in an unbroken stream.

Of all the teachings given by Atisha in Tibet, the *lojong* cycle from Serlingpa is considered the most quintessential. This cycle of instructions are prized by all schools of Tibetan Buddhism, and have profoundly influenced the sentiment of Tibetan spirituality in general. Over the centuries we Tibetans have drawn strength, courage and joy from the precious *lojong* instruction.

The specific lineage of *Seven Points for Training the Mind* was originally passed only to small groups of disciples. However, some generations later one of the Kadampa lamas, Geshey Chekhawa by name, transcribed them in order to ensure their preservation.   From his time to the present day, the brief text of *Lojong Dondunma* that he created has been a source of constant inspiration to Tibetan writers, and many commentaries to it have appeared in all Tibetan schools.   These differ in length, style and focus; but they are all equally infused with the vast and profound advice that Serlingpa gives us.

The First Dalai Lama began his formal spiritual life as a prenovice monk in Nartang, a monastery of the school directly descending from Atisha.   Therefore, from a very young age he was immersed in the *lojong* teachings.   His biography emphasizes the attention he gave to the study and practice of them.   His 'Collected Works' contain two commentaries to Geshey Chekhawa's *Seven Points for Training the Mind:* the first being a brief text in the form of notes; and the second a longer and more traditional treatment. This second work is known in Tibetan as *Tekchen Lojong,* or *Training the Mind on the Great Way.* The First Dalai Lama composed it in the mid-fifteenth century by the Western calendar, so it is of considerable antiquity. The essential message of the *lojong* teaching is that if we want to see a better world, we should begin by improving our own mind.   This was said by the Indian master Shantideva, who pointed out that there are two ways to make the world a comfortable place in which to walk. One way is to cover the world with leather; the other is to put on some shoes.

Similarly, we can spend our life trying to 'tame' the world, a task that would never end; or we can take the more practical path of 'taming' our own minds.   The latter is by far the more effective approach, and brings the most immediate, stable and lasting solution. It contributes to our own inner happiness, and also contributes to establishing an atmosphere of peace and harmony in the world around us.

As the Buddha has said, "The Mind is the forerunner of all events."   One way of understanding this line is that if our mind is positive, then our activities of body and speech, and thus our lifestyle, immediately become positive.   This automatically renders them conducive to happiness for ourselves and those around us.   On the other hand when the mind is negative, then our activities of body and speech, and thus our lifestyle, become negative.   This automatically contributes to frustration and unhappiness for ourselves and others.

Not only does the state of our mind dramatically affect the way in which we choose to shape our future, it also significantly influences the manner in which we experience the present moment. For example, a person with a well-trained mind can experience the greatest external hardship with very little disturbance to his or her inner peace and happiness, whereas someone with an untrained mind may find even the smallest inconvenience to be a great disturbance to inner peace.

I have often pointed out to Tibetans that the *lojong* teaching is one of the principal sources of our strength as a people. It has helped us tremendously over the recent decades of hardship and suffering brought upon us by the Chinese invasion and brutal occupation of our homeland. I advise my people that if we rely upon the ideals of compassion and wisdom as taught in our spiritual traditions for so many centuries, and as expressed so well in the *lojong* teaching, then nothing the Chinese military does to us can harm us. In the end we will endure and succeed. On the other hand, if we give up the spiritual ideals that have characterized us as a people for so long, values that we as a culture can bring into the modern world as our small contribution to world civilization, then even if we win our struggle for self-determination we will have suffered a greater loss.

The First Dalai Lama's *lojong* commentary illustrates the commitment to the ideals of love, compassion and wisdom that characterized Tibetan Buddhism when he composed his work some five-and-a-half centuries ago. And although sometimes the forms of his expression may not completely suit modern sensitivities, the essence of his message remains relevant. This essence is that if we ourselves wish to contribute to an enlightened world, the way to begin is by cultivating our minds.

This is the meaning of the Tibetan word *lojong*. Here *lo* means mind, and *jong* means to train or transform. In other words, we need to train the mind in the bodhisattva ways, in the practices that induce the qualities of kindness, love, compassion, tolerance, inner strength, wisdom, and so forth. When we do that, we immediately become happier and more balanced people, and we contribute to happiness and harmony around us.

At present the world is not lacking in the technology of war. Our weapons of destruction are everywhere, and more are being produced every day, their sophistication and power constantly increasing. But what we are lacking is the technology of peace, the technology to produce love, kindness, and open-heartedness. Material development is useful and necessary, but unless linked to a corresponding development of humane spiritual vision it will not only be useless, but also harmful and counter-productive to the achievement of happiness during our life on this earth.   The destruction of the environment and the extinction of numerous forms of wildlife are examples of how material technology devoid of spiritual sensitivity can have disastrous results.

The *lojong* teachings of the illustrious Indonesian master Serlingpa, quintessential presentations of the key teachings of Buddha, have proven beneficial to Central Asians for almost a thousand years now.   They may also offer a few suggestions relevant to the modern world.   Some of the *lojong* ideas may seem limited to a specific time and situation; but the essence carries a timeless message.   This message recommends that we transcend spiritual pettiness and ego-centric behavior, and instead learn to see ourselves in the context of a commitment to universal responsibility.   We have to look less at what we can grab for ourselves from this world and from others, and more at how we can be useful in a universal sense.

Greed has no end, and from the beginning produces no happiness. This was expressed by the holy Indian master Shantideva, when he wrote, "The buddhas care only for others; worldly beings care only for themselves. Just look at the difference between the two."   If we can become more like the former, like the buddhas and bodhisattvas, then we ourselves will become the immediate and direct beneficaries of the consequent spiritual rewards. Others benefit indirectly.

I myself received the *lojong* teachings of holy Serlingpa when still a child, and have used them as the basis of my practice since that time. I include the *lojong* methods of meditation for cultivating the spirit of love and compassion in my own daily devotions, and have greatly benefited from them.   There are several *lojong* texts that I memorized as a child, and I still recite these every day.

For me, the *lojong* tradition stands as the heart of the Buddha's message of peace.   It teaches us how to regard others with the dignity and care that they deserve, and also how to transcend the limitations of conventional ego-grasping.   In brief, it is a guideline for our own enlightenment, leading to enlightened conduct in our dealings with others.

The benefits of studying the *lojong* tradition come not merely in the intellectual understanding of the meditative techniques that it suggests, but in the actual application of those meditations. Many of these are methods that can be practiced not just by Buddhists, but by anyone with a commitment to developing a good heart.   We all need love and compassion, whether we are Buddhist or not, inclined to spiritual practice or not, formally religious or not.   Kindness is a universal need, and it is something that we all appreciate being shown.

I offer my prayers that an English translation of the First Dalai Lama's important text on *lojong* may contribute to the spirit of love and kindness in this world, and to an understanding of the rich spiritual heritage that once existed in the Land of Snow Mountains.

10 May 1991

Translator's Introduction

I. ATISHA AND THE *LOJONG* SPIRITUAL LEGACY

One of the last truly great Indian Buddhist masters to teach widely in Tibet was Dipamkara Shrijnana, popularly known simply as Atisha, 'The Master.'

This illustrious monk, born in Bengal in 982 A.D., arrived in the Land of Snows in 1042 and remained there until his death some thirteen years later. His work left an impression that profoundly influenced the character of Tibetan Buddhism.[1]

The teachings that he delivered to the Tibetans, especially those in the cycle of "oral transmissions" (Tib., Man-ngag), even today rank amongst the most highly revered and popular subjects for public discourse by the lamas of all the various sects. For example, His Holiness the present Dalai Lama often uses one of the early lineages emanating from Atisha as the basis of his public discourses.

Of the many oral transmission teachings that Atisha gave to the Tibetans, the most essential are those in the cycle of *lojong* (Tib., bLo-sbyong), or "Direct Methods for Training the Mind." Moreover, the most important of all his lojong teachings is that famed as the *Lojong Dondunma* (Tib., bLo-sbyong-don-bdun-ma), or "Seven Points for Training the Mind." It is this tradition that is the focus of the commentary by the First Dalai Lama translated in this volume, *Training the Mind in the Great Way.*[2]

As the First Dalai Lama points out in the opening section of his commentary, "Atisha had received three lines of the lojong transmission: one from the (Indonesian) master Serlingpa (Tib., gSer-gling-pa), another from the (Indian) master Maitriyogi, and the third from his (Indian) guru Dharmarakshita. . . . The tradition to be dealt with here. . . is the oral tradition teaching for training the mind on the Great Way through the techniques of exchanging self-cherishing for the cherishing of others, and is the lojong tradition that Atisha received from his teacher Serlingpa."

Not a great deal is known about Atisha's Indonesian master. There are several Tibetan biographies of him, but these are generally quite brief. It is said that he was born a prince in the Indonesian city of Shrivijaya. At the time Indonesia was a great Buddhist center, famed in India for its generous patronage of the Buddhist arts.

Following in the footsteps of the Buddha, who also had been born a prince and became a homeless religious mendicant, Serlingpa as a youth became a Buddhist monk and traveled to India to study the holy Dharma. There he trained under many of the most qualified teachers of the era and eventually achieved a high level of realization. His ordination name was Dharmakirti, though he is not to be confused with the famous Indian logician of the same name. Tibetans prefer to refer to him simply as Serlingpa, literally, "he of the Golden Islands," that is, "the Indonesian."

In the later phase of his life Serlingpa returned to his homeland to teach to his own people. Yet his fame as a great spiritual master endured in India, and when Atisha heard stories of him he decided to undertake the dangerous sea journey to Indonesia in order to study under him. In fact he remained at Serlingpa's feet for twelve years and came to regard him as the most important of the fifty spiritual masters under whom he had studied. Many years later in Tibet tears would come to his eyes whenever he referred to this enlightened sage.

After twelve years in Indonesia Atisha returned to India and taught the Dharma there until eventually he came to Tibet. The story of Atisha's coming to Tibet is particularly moving. It is said that the king of Western Tibet, Yeshe Od (Tib., Ye-shes-od) had sent several requests to the Indian Buddhist elders requesting that Atisha be sent to teach in Tibet. However, as Atisha was regarded as India's greatest spiritual master these requests were declined.

Some years later King Yeshe Od fell into the hands of an enemy army, who held him to ransom for the weight of his body in gold. When his nephew came with the ransom and the gold was weighed, it was discovered that the sum was short by the amount equal in weight to Yeshe Od's head.

The king took his nephew aside and made a dramatic request. "I am an old man, and anyway shall soon die," he said. "Take the gold to India and offer it to Atisha's monastery. Tell the elders that our request for Atisha comes with this gold, and also with the head of a king."

Thus it came to pass that Atisha was allowed to leave his monastery in India and go to teach in Tibet.

From the historical point of view it is significant that he did. Within the next two centuries Muslim invaders swept over the Indian subcontinent, through the Malaysian peninsula and into Indonesia, destroying Buddhism in their wake. Meanwhile, the enlightenment lineages of Atisha were safely preserved in the Land of Snows. In fact, although many aspects of Indian Buddhism have been preserved in countries such as Shri Lanka, Thailand, China, Japan and so forth, it seems that only in Tibet have the unique Indonesian Buddhist lineages survived.[3]

Atisha taught in Tibet for the remainder of his life, and during that time guided thousands of disciples along the enlightenment path. Of all of them, his greatest student was the layman Lama Drom Tonpa (Tib., bLa-ma-'brom-ston-pa), who is regarded as a previous incarnation of the Dalai Lamas. It was not to his many monk disciples, but to the layman Lama Drom that Atisha passed his most important lineages. Lama Drom Tonpa then transmitted the legacy to his chief disciples, and so on down the generations.[4]

The Thirteenth Dalai Lama succinctly summarized the content and the early history of Atisha's lineages in his New Year sermon of the Fire Dragon Year (1926). I quote him here from my study of his life and teachings, *Path of the Bodhisattva Warrior:*[5]

Atisha widely taught the Buddhadharma in Tibet. Later his chief disciple Lama Drom Tonpa organized his transmissions into the legacy known as "The Four Divinities and Three Dharmas," a tradition whereby an individual practitioner could perceive all doctrines of the sutras and tantras as non-contradictory and could personally apply them all as complementary methods for the accomplishment of enlightenment. The lineage eventually came to be known as "Atisha's Kadam Tradition, the Marvellous Legacy of Seven Divine Dharmas."

Lama Drom transmitted the various lineages of Atisha by dividing them between "the three Kadampa brothers." To one he gave the scriptural traditions, to the second the oral transmissions, and to the third the pith instructions.

The scriptural traditions were of two main types: those dealing with ultimate reality and the wisdom of emptiness; and those dealing with conventional reality and the vast bodhimind activities.

As for the former of these, or those dealing with the ultimate wisdom of emptiness, the principal texts stressed here were Nagarjuna's six treatises on emptiness philosophy, such as *The Root of Wisdom* (Skt., *Mulamadhyamika-karika*) and so forth, together with the commentaries to them by the later Indian masters; and also Atisha's own commentaries on the middle view and on the nature of the two truths.

Six quintessential texts were used to elucidate the nature of the bodhisattva's vast activities: *The Bodhi-*

sattva Stages (Skt., *Bodhisattvabhumi*); *An Ornament of Mahayana Sutras* (Skt., *Mahayanasutra-alamkara*); *A Compendium of Bodhisattva Trainings* (Skt., *Shikshasamucchaya*); *A Guide to the Bodhisattva Way* (Skt., *Bodhisattvacharya-avatara*); *A Garland of Birth Stories* (Skt., *Jatakamala*); and *Collected Sayings of the Buddha* (Skt., *Udanavarga*). It is the tradition to read from the fifth of these, *A Garland of Birth Stories*, during the morning session of the Great Prayer Festival.

These were the principal scriptures studied in the Old Kadam School.

As for the oral transmission teachings, these emanated from and were the essential practices taught in the above scriptures. These oral tradition teachings are generally known as "the instructions for training the mind in the Mahayana tradition" (Tib., Theg-chen-blo-sbyong-gi-gdampa-pa).

Atisha had collected these lojong teachings from his three principal Indian gurus, and also from his master Serlingpa. He then secretly transmitted them to his chief disciple, Lama Drom Tonpa.

During the time of the three Kadampa brothers many of these oral teachings were collected together and compiled into the text *Stages of the Doctrine* (Tib., *sTan-rim*). Yet at the time the lineages from his Indonesian master were still kept secret.

However, these too eventually were publicly revealed when the times were sufficiently mature. First Geshe Khamlungpa published *Eight Sessions for Training the Mind* (Tib., *bLo-sbyong-thun-brgyad-ma*). Then Geshe Langri Tangpa wrote *Eight Verses for Training the Mind* (Tib., *bLo-sbyong-tshig-brgyad-ma*). After this Sangye Gompa composed *A Public Explanation* (Tib., *Tshogs-bshad-ma*) and Geshe Chekhawa wrote *Seven Points for Training the Mind* (Tib., *bLo-sbyong-don-bdun-ma*).

In this way the lojong oral transmission teachings gradually emerged. Later all these were brought together into the anthology *A Hundred Texts on Training the Mind* (Tib., *bLo-byong-brgya-rtsa*).

As for the third lineage transmitted by Lama Drom—that of the pith instructions—this has its root in the secret oral teachings of Atisha and his disciples as embodied in *The Great Book of the Kadampa Masters: A Jewel Rosary of Profound Instructions on the Bodhisattva Way* (Tib., *bKa'-gdams-glegs-bam-chen-mo-zab-tshig-byang-chub-sems-dpa'-nor-bui-phreng-ba*). . . .

Of the above lineages of transmission, it is the lojong formulation of Geshe Chekhawa (Tib., dGe-bshes-'chad-kha-ba), known as *Seven Points for Training the Mind*, in which we are most interested, for it is this lineage that is used as the "root text" by the First Dalai Lama in the work translated in this volume. In other words, it is to the meditative tradition coming from Atisha and transcribed by Geshe Chekhawa as the brief text of *Seven Points for Training the Mind* that the Dalai Lama directs his commentary. Moreover, it is this formulation of the lojong tradition, received by Atisha from his Indonesian master Serlingpa and widely propagated in Tibet, that is considered to be the most important of all the lojong presentations of the path.

It should be noted that there are a number of different versions of Geshe Chekhawa's text on *Seven Points for Training the Mind*. These do not substantially vary in content; but they do exhibit a different order of the lines, and some versions seem to contain a few additional words.

I asked several lineage holders, including His Holiness the Dalai Lama and the abbot of the Dalai Lama's monastery, Denma Lochö Rinpoche, for their thoughts on the matter. The general view seems to be that individual commentators have the liberty to somewhat rearrange the text as a means of enhancing their presentation of ideas; they also are at liberty to take in passages from other original lojong works, such as those mentioned above by the Thirteenth Dalai Lama. However, it is not my purpose here to bring out a critical edition of Geshe

Chekhawa's root text, so I did not pursue the matter further. For those who are interested, the extensive commentary by the Eighth Dalai Lama's guru Kachen Yeshe Gyaltsen (Tib., bKa'-chen-ye-shes-rgyal-mtshan) goes into the subject in considerable detail.[6]

The First Dalai Lama in fact wrote two commentaries to Geshe Chekhawa's *Seven Points*. Readers will note that the root texts used in the two do show some variations. Neither commentary gives a reason for the specific arrangement of lines that is followed.

I included the shorter of these two commentaries in my study on the life and works of the First Dalai Lama, *Bridging the Sutras and Tantras*.[7] The text translated in this volume is the longer commentary, and is approximately two and a half times the length of the shorter one.

II. THE NATURE OF THE LOJONG PRACTICE

It may be useful at this point to say something about the character of the lojong tradition as a method of spiritual practice.

The principal feature of the lojong approach is that it identifies the obstacles to enlightenment as being twofold. The first of these is *chezin* (Tib., bces-'dzin), or the self-cherishing attitude, the habit of always placing ourselves above others and of working to benefit ourselves at others' expense. This is the great mischief-maker that brings conflict and disharmony into our world and that causes us to harm others. It is the greatest single enemy to our peace of mind.

The second obstacle is *dakzin* (Tib., bdag-'dzin), or ego-grasping, the I-holding ignorance. This refers to the instinctive belief in a truly existent self, the grasping attitude of seeing something independent and truly existent within ourselves and external phenomena.

The second of the above two obstacles is in fact deeper than the first, for were it not for the I-grasping habit, self-cherishing would not arise. Nonetheless both must be identified and counteracted, for both are constantly creating problems for us.

The lojong method inspires enlightenment within us by eliminating these two syndromes and by replacing them respectively with great compassion and the blissful wisdom of emptiness.

The lojong approach for eliminating these two obstacles is known as the method for cultivating the two types of *bodhichitta*, or enlightenment mind: the conventional bodhimind of love and compassion, and the ultimate bodhimind of the wisdom of emptiness. The techniques for cultivating these two bodhiminds constitute the main substance of the lojong training. In the seven-point lojong system, this is the second of the seven points. The other six points firstly prepare one for and then support and sustain this "actual practice."

Thus in the sevenfold scheme the first point is the preliminary trainings; the second is the actual practice of cultivating the two bodhiminds; the third is the method of using the bodhimind techniques to transform hardships and challenges into aids on the path to enlightenment; the fourth is the method of integrating the trainings throughout one's life and also at the time of death; the fifth is the way to observe for the signs of progress; the sixth is the commitments of the training; and the seventh is general advice to practitioners.

One of my late teachers, the Ven. Lama Tubten Yeshe, summarized the nature of the lojong tradition very succinctly, and I would like to quote his words here. Some readers may have met this wonderful man, for he traveled and taught extensively throughout the Western world during the final decade of his life. Others may have read about or heard of him, as after he passed away his *tulku* (Tib., sPrul-sku), or official reincarnation, was recognized in the person of a young Spanish child, Tenzin Osel Torres, who received considerable attention from the international media. A few years before his death Lama Tubten Yeshe had provided me with a preface to *Bridging the Sutras and Tantras*. As this collection contained the First Dalai Lama's short commentary to the *Seven Point* lojong tradition Lama Yeshe spoke on the subject. His eloquent words are just as relevant to the First Dalai Lama's longer commentary, which is the focus of this text, so it is not inappropriate for me to repeat them here:

Gendun Drup's commentary to the Atisha tradition of seven points to train the mind, or lojong, provides advice particularly useful for our day-to-day life. It is neither exotic nor poetic, but purely pragmatic: its subject is how to transform one's every activity into a method of opening the heart toward others. This is right livelihood, right action, in the deeper sense of the words.

Especially in the present age of social and economic unrest, when so few conditions encourage spiritual practice and so many oppose it, when the use of material resources, which are meant to support life, is exaggerated to obsession, the lojong teaching is most useful. To live we must use material things, but at present the world has largely degenerated into seeing material grasping as the supreme answer to existence.

This is the environment in which we ourselves must live and practice. Lojong is a method very effective in transforming aggressive and grasping circumstances into aids on the path. Unless we have a method that can be applied in every situation, it will be very difficult to tame the wild elephant of the mind in this twentieth century.

Another important aspect of the lojong teaching is that it is practiced by all four sects of Tibetan Buddhism. The lineage was originally brought to Tibet by Atisha in the mid-eleventh century and formed the basis of the ancient Kadam tradition, but from the Kadampa teachers it gradually found its way into all four Tibetan sects. Many commentaries to it can be found in the writings of all Tibetan orders. This wide-range applicability of the lojong teaching in Tibet is doubly relevant, for it means that not only is the First

Dalai Lama's commentary acceptable to all students of Tibetan Buddhism regardless of sect, a certain universality of the lojong doctrine is suggested. As well as being of value to all traditions of Buddhism, it can be used and applied by all people interested in true spiritual development. Whether or not one is a Buddhist, whether or not one believes in the traditional interpretations of Buddha, Dharma and Sangha, whether or not one is formally religious, the lojong teaching can be beneficially implemented.

III. THE TIBETAN BACKGROUND

It is not possible to state with precision exactly when Buddhism began to find its way into the Tibetan regions. But we can conjecture that, located only a few hundred miles to the north of Buddha Shakyamuni's birthplace of Lumbini, the Tibetans certainly must have been aware to some degree of the Buddhist tradition from the very earliest of times. David Snellgrove, commenting on the history of the ancient pre-Buddhist religions of Tibet, writes, "Buddhist hermits and yogins, and probably Hindu ascetics as well, had already familiarized the villages of Western Tibet with Indian teachings and practices long before Buddhism was formally introduced by the Tibetan religious kings.... Moreover, these 'informal' contacts continued over many centuries."[8]

Indeed, according to one popular legend Tibet's first king was an exiled Indian prince, the fifth son of a famous Buddhist patron, King Prasenajit of Magadha.[9]

This prince, the story goes, was somewhat deformed at birth, and felt shunned by his father and elder brothers. Consequently when he came of age he ran away from home. Eventually he found his way into the Yarlung Valley southeast of Lhasa, where he greatly impressed the Tibetans with his refined appearance and his gentle demeanor. They adopted him into their community, and in the end he became their chieftain. They gave him the name Nyatri Tsenpo (Tib., gNya'-khri-btsan-po),

"The Palanquin-borne Lord," by which he is known to history. Tibetan culture took a dramatic turn in the mid-seventh century under the rule of King Songtsen Gampo (Tib., Srong-btsan-sgam-po). This ruler married five wives, the first of whom was a Buddhist princess from Nepal. In her honor Songtsen Gampo built the Jokhang Temple, destined to become Tibet's holiest shrine. The main gate of the building faced south toward her homeland. In addition, he ordered the construction of 108 minor Buddhist temples and monuments at sites around Lhasa to propitiate the spirits of the land.

A few years later Songtsen Gampo took another foreign wife, this time a Buddhist princess from China. For her too he constructed a temple, the Ramoche. Its main entrance faced eastward, toward the place of her birth.

These two Buddhist wives seem to have had a more spiritual effect upon the king than did his three Tibetan consorts, for he himself soon embraced the Buddhadharma with an enthusiasm and vigor that transformed his country's cultural landscape. He delegated a large number of his court intellectuals to visit India and study the Dharma there, and to create a blueprint for the translation of Buddhist books into Tibetan. A new script was formulated, based on a Kashmiri version of Sanskrit, and numerous dictionaries were compiled.

Songtsen Gampo's work made a quantum leap forward a century later under his descendent King Trisong Deutsen (Tib., Khri-srong-lde-btsan), who invited a large number of Indian masters to the Land of Snows in an effort to systematically translate the Indian scriptures, create a full-fledged monastery, and establish a sangha. Among the most esteemed of the masters to teach in Tibet at the time were Guru Padmasambhava and Shantirakshita, who jointly oversaw the construction of Samye, the country's first monastery.

The final landmark in Tibet's early religious history occurred in 792 A.D. Two principal streams of Buddhism had emerged to dominate the Tibetan scene: that coming from India, which represented a blend of the classical Mahayana and Vajrayana lineages; and that from China, consisting of an aspect of the

Mahayana as filtered through and characterized by the Taoist sentiment. These two, concluded the Lhasa intellectuals of the time, were incompatible both philosophically and in practical application; one of them would have to go.

A grand assembly was convened, and a formal debate announced. Kamalashila was summoned from India to represent the Indian tradition; a monk by the name of Hoshang Mahayana would represent the Chinese. As the story goes, the latter lost so decisively that he had to flee from Lhasa while the Tibetans pelted him with dirty socks, stones and similar paraphernalia.

The outcome was dramatic. Chinese Buddhism was henceforth banned from the Land of Snows, as was the translation of Chinese literature into Tibetan. Even the use of the Chinese script was outlawed. Chinese monks would be allowed to visit Tibet to study Buddhism, but not to teach. For better or worse the die was cast, and Tibetan Buddhism would henceforth take its inspiration solely from the sages of India.

Over the generations that followed a large number of Indian masters were invited to Tibet to teach and translate scriptures. Also, numerous Tibetan scholar/monks traveled to the monasteries and hermitages of India to learn Sanskrit and master the subtleties of Buddhist thought.

The various lineages of Buddhism that trace directly to these early beginnings are generally referred to as the *Nyingma* (Tib., rNying-ma), or "Old School." They are characterized by a similarity in style of terminology, due largely to the fact that they are based on translations made in accordance with the dictionaries and guidelines set forth by the translation teams patronized by the early kings.

In the mid-eleventh century the Land of Snows blossomed forth in a grand renaissance. Large numbers of Tibetan masters began to revise and rework many of the old translations, using new and upgraded lexicons. Three new schools formed during this period: the Sakya (Tib., Sa-skya), Kargyu (Tib., dKa'-rgyud), and Kadam (Tib., dKa'-gdams). It was the last of these three schools, the illustrious Kadam, that had its roots directly and exclusively in the fertile soil of the lineages of Atisha.

Yet the teachings of Atisha were quickly to pass beyond the confines of the Kadam order. Within a generation they had been adopted by both the Sakya and Kargyu, and have since remained as major components of these orders. Before long they also were absorbed by the Nyingma, being incorporated by the thirteenth-century reformer Longchen Rabjampa (Tib., kLong-chen-rab-'byams-pa) into his classical treatises on Nyingma doctrine, and were consequently wholeheartedly embraced by most later Nyingma writers.

The year 1357 saw the birth of a man in Eastern Tibet who was to have a dramatic and far-reaching impact on Tibetan religious history: Lama Tsongkhapa (Tib., bLa-ma-gtsong-kha-pa, 1357-1419), the founder of the Gelukpa order (Tib., dGe-lugs).

The Gelukpa sect was considerably different from the earlier schools of Tibetan Buddhism. Each of the earlier schools traced its root directly to India, and usually to the lineages of one or two Indian masters. The Gelukpa, on the other hand, was Tibet's first eclectic movement. Rather than serve as a "new" school of Tibetan Buddhism born from a separate Indian root, it was a synthesis of all the earlier schools. Lama Tsongkhapa had studied with some forty-five teachers from all the Tibetan schools. He saw his mission as being that of bringing under one roof the best of them all.

He was certainly successful, if we are to measure him from the viewpoint of the popularity he achieved. Within a few generations of his passing the Gelukpas had become as large as all the older schools combined.

In combining and fusing the best of Tibet's spiritual lineages, however, Tsongkhapa chose to take as his philosophical and spiritual foundations the teachings of Atisha and his Kadam tradition. All other lineages drawn into the Geluk were placed within the overall structure of the Kadampa perspective, and were recast in the Kadampa mold.

For this reason the Geluk is sometimes referred to in Tibetan histories as the Kadam Sarma (Tib., bKa'-gdams-gsar-ma), or the "New Kadam Order." It soon absorbed almost all the Old Kadam monasteries, as well as inspiring the creation of new monasteries and nunneries of its own.

The First Dalai Lama was the youngest of Tsongkhapa's five chief disciples. But history was soon to make him the most visible of the five, and the most important from the perspective of the widespread success that the Geluk order achieved.

IV. THE FIRST DALAI LAMA

The First Dalai Lama was born in 1391 as the son of tribal nomadic herdsmen in the Tsang region of southwestern Tibet. At the time Tibet was a land in which Buddhism flourished in every region of the country, where every valley contained numerous monasteries, nunneries or spiritual hermitages.

His father died when he was in his seventh year, and his mother, too poor to support him on her own, placed him in Nartang Monastery under the care of a kindly uncle, Geshe Choshe (Tib., dGe-bshes-chos-bshad) by name. Nartang Monastery was associated with Atisha's Kadam tradition, so from a young age he trained in the Kadampa path to enlightenment.

The child's profoundly spiritual nature did not pass unnoticed, and soon he became a personal disciple of Nartang's great abbot, Druppa Sherab (Tib., Grub-pa-shes-rab). It was from this master that he received his higher monastic ordination, and from whom he received the name by which he has become known to history, Gendun Druppa (Tib., dGe-'dun-grub-pa).

As an adult Gendun Druppa traveled throughout central and southern Tibet studying with a wide range of teachers and dedicating himself to the practice of meditation. He met Lama Tsongkhapa in 1415, four years before the latter was to pass away. The meeting must have been moving for both of them; it is said that Tsongkhapa tore a piece of cloth from one of his robes and gave it to the young monk as a symbol of passing his essential lineages to him, prophesying that the latter would become an important teacher and monastic elder in his later life.

From this time on the First Dalai Lama always regarded Lama Tsongkhapa as his innermost spiritual guide, and after Tsongkhapa passed away the youth spent several years in the Lhasa area gathering all of Tsongkhapa's lineages into himself. Eventually he came to be regarded as the greatest living master in the Geluk Order, an unsurpassed holder of Je Tsongkhapa's lineages. As is mentioned by the First Dalai Lama in the opening pages of the text translated in this volume, he bases his commentary on an oral discourse given by Lama Tsongkhapa to Lama Namkha Paldenpa (Tib., bLa-ma-nam-mkha'-dpal-ldan-pa). The first Dalai Lama himself then received the lineage from the latter guru, some years after Lama Tsongkhapa had passed away.

For some reason a large number of Western writers seem to have confused the roles of Lama Tsongkhapa, the First Dalai Lama's guru, with that of Geshe Choshe, his uncle and guardian while he was a child in Nartang Monastery. The meticulous Stephen Batchelor even makes the mistake in his *Tibet Guide*.[10] He perhaps derives his wrong understanding from the works of earlier historians such as Hoffman and Stein, who mis-inform us that "Tsongkhapa's greatest disciple and heir was his nephew Gendun Druppa."

The truth is quite to the contrary. The emphasis in Tsongkhapa's syncretic movement, and one of the reasons that it achieved such a high level of both spirituality and popular support, was that it disengaged itself from such feudal practices as hereditary succession of spiritual authority, a tradition that at the time was all too common with the older sects of Tibetan Buddhism. In the newly formed Gelukpa order, the criteria for success were nothing other than academic and spiritual excellence. In fact it is possible that Gendun Druppa's great popularity with the masses of Central Asia may have been empowered by the fact that he began his monastic career as an impoverished semi-orphan from a remote region of Southern Tibet; his obscure background perhaps made his spiritual accomplishments all the more striking.

Gendun Druppa's fame as a spiritual master soon pervaded the Land of Snows. No longer was he the simple monk of nomadic parentage. Throughout the last half of his life he served as one of the most beloved spiritual teachers in Central Asia, known simply by the name of Tamche Khyenpa (Tib., Thamscad-mkhyen-pa), "The Omniscient One." Kings and tribal chieftains bowed to him for his teachings, and the highest lamas came to him in search of instruction and initiation.

Usually the dates of Gendun Druppa's life are given as 1391-1474, due to the tradition Western historians have of matching Tibetan and Western yearly cycles. In fact the Tibetan new year begins with the new moon of February, so occasionally a problem arises (i.e., with anything occurring in the last few weeks of the Tibetan year). Gendun Druppa passed away on the half-moon day of the twelfth month of the Wood Horse Year, that is, three weeks before the new moon of February 1475.

He established a number of monasteries during his lifetime, the most important of which was Tashi Lhunpo (Tib., bKrashis-lhun-po) near the town of Shigatse, Southern Tibet. This monastery was eventually to become one of the four greatest monastic universities of Central Asia, and still stands today as an exquisite example of classical Tibetan art and archecture.

One of the major biographies of him, *The Twelve Marvellous Deeds in the Life of the Omniscient Gendun Druppa* (Tib., *mNgo-mtsar-mdzes-pa-bcu-gnyis*) describes his passing as follows:[11]

On the seventh day of the middle month of winter he summoned Dulzinpa Sempa Chenpo and the other great teachers of Tashi Lhunpo to him. These are the words he spoke to them.

"Exert yourselves in the spiritual activities constituting the path to enlightenment. Although I would like to remain with you forever, the time of my passing is near. But this is not the cause of regret; it is simply the workings of the natural law of death. After I have passed away there is no need to perform elaborate rituals for me nor to build an elaborate tomb for my remains.... If you are devoted to me and feel that my work here has been of benefit to you, then after I have passed away you should remain in Tashi Lhunpo and work for the good of the monastery and the preservation and dissemination of the holy Dharma...."

In the first watch of the night he performed the generation stage meditations of Highest Yoga Tantra.... At midnight he slept for a short while, and then during the last watch of night he arose and engaged in meditation upon the completion stage yogas. Here he entered into the practice of the tantric method of breath meditation known as 'vajra recitation,' and by means of this technique established the absorption of the yoga of four voidnesses.

Thus at dawn on the eighth day (half moon) of the twelfth month of the Wood Horse Year, when the master was in his eighty-fourth year, he manifested the external signs of dissolving into the four voidnesses, manifesting clear light realization and abiding in the state of *Dharmakaya* wisdom. Thus his attainment of perfection was made evident.

For thirty days after Gendun Druppa's passing, until the full moon of the new year, an utter stillness presided over the area. The earth and its waters became warmed, and the leaves of the trees turned their faces downward. The sky remained completely clear, without a cloud or even a bird to disturb its stillness. These and many other such signs filled the world in order to demonstrate to one and all the passing of a sage who had achieved the highest knowledge.

The First Dalai Lama was a prolific writer. His official *Collected Works* (Tib., *gSung-'bum*) amounts to six thick volumes and contains dozens of titles. As mentioned above, I included sixteen of these related to essential spiritual subjects in my study of his life and works.

His other major writings largely focus upon philosophical subjects suggested by classical Indian Buddhism, such as *pramana, madhyamaka, abhidharma,* and so forth. Most of these are still studied today, and are written in the form of commentaries to classical Indian treatises, including the principal works of Indian sages such as Nagarjuna, Chandrakirti, Vasubandhu, Dharmakirti, and so others.

He is also particularly famous for his writings on *vinaya,* or the monastic way of life. In addition, his devotional poetry is considered to stand with the best to come out of Central Asia.

Less than a year after the First Dalai Lama passed away a child was born in Southern Tibet who eventually came to be recognized as the reincarnation of Gendun Druppa, "The Omniscient One." He was reinstated in Tashi Lhunpo Monastery and grew up to become one of the greatest lamas and spiritual teachers of his age, Gyalwa Gendun Gyatso (Tib., rGyal-ba-dge-'dun-rgya-mtsho). By the time he passed away in 1542 his fame outshone that of any other Tibetan sage.

In turn, after he passed away another child was identified and reinstated as the incarnation of Gendun Druppa. This was the third incarnation, Gyalwa Sonam Gyatso.

It was this third incarnation of the line who was the first to be known by the name of "Dalai Lama." The first two had been called Tamche Khyenpa, "The Omniscient One." Gyalwa Sonam Gyatso was invited to Mongolia in 1578 in order to teach the great king Altan Khan. The Mongol king took the last part of his name, or "Gyatso," meaning "Ocean," and rendered it into Mongolian. Thus it became "Talai," later vernacularized by the British as "Dalai." To the Tibetans he has always remained "Tamche Khyenpa"; but to the Mongols and later to the Chinese, and in more recent centuries to Westerners, he became "the Dalai Lama," that is, "Teacher (vast as the) Ocean." The present incarnation is the fourteenth in the line.

V. A NOTE ON THE TEXTUAL RENDITION

Some years ago I translated the shorter of the First Dalai Lama's two commentaries to *Seven Points for Training the Mind* and included it in my volume on the life and writings of that great teacher. The edition contained a collection of sixteen texts written by the First Dalai Lama on various quintessential spiritual topics, as well as a biographical profile on him.

The brief lojong treatise included therein was written in the form of notes taken by a disciple at a public discourse given by the First Dalai Lama on the root text of the *Seven Points*, and was entitled *Notes on Spiritual Transformation* (Tib., *bLo-sbyong-zin-'bris*). It seemed more appropriate to a literary collection (than was the longer commentary) due to the informality of its style and also because of its brevity.

However, over the years to follow I kept returning to the longer commentary. Its clarity of expression, simplicity of style and attention to detail, as well as its inspired treatment of the meditations on love, compassion and the conventional *bodhichitta*, or bodhisattva aspiration, seemed to me to place it among the greatest spiritual testaments ever to appear in Tibetan literature. It also contains one of the most exhaustive treatments of the topic of taking refuge that I have seen in any work of this nature.

In 1982 I read the main body of the work with one of my lamas, the gentle Chomdzey Tashi Wangyal, a *geshe* of Drepung Loseling Monastery who was working as a research scholar at the Dalai Lama's Library of Tibetan Works and Archives in Dharamsala, India. Chomdzey-la, a monk from the Kham region of East Tibet, lives and breathes the classical Kadampa tradition taught by Atisha. His profound commentary brought an exquisite vitality into the pages of the First Dalai Lama's text, rendering lucent the various shades and subtleties of meaning. Shortly thereafter I prepared a draft translation based on that reading.

However, the work was to sit on the shelf for quite some time. Although over the years to follow I would pick it up and dabble with it every few months or so, there never seemed to be the time or energy to carry it from a draft translation to a final manuscript. Yet the First Dalai Lama's extensive lojong commentary never ventured far from my thoughts. In my mind it had the makings of a Buddhist classic, and its translation was a seed in the process of maturation. As time passed the intent to see it reach fruition remained with me.

Finally in the spring of 1990, I found myself in Dharamsala once more, with no specific demands on my time. My old lama friend Chomdzey Tashi Wangyal was also there, still in the employ of the Tibetan Library. I approached him to re-read the First Dalai Lama's text with me and help me iron out any rough edges and points of doubt. He readily agreed, and off we went.

As fortune would have it the Ladakhi lama Rizong Tulku was also in Dharamsala at the time to receive some transmissions from H.H. the Dalai Lama. Rizong Tulku, a former abbot of both the Gyumey Tantric College and Drepung Loseling Monastery, is regarded as one of the greatest living masters of the lojong literary tradition. He agreed to help resolve any uncertain passages. As the First Dalai Lama's text was composed more than five hundred years ago it contains a number of antique terms and phrases; Ven. Rizong Tulku had no difficulty elucidating these for us. Each day I was able to give eight or ten hours to the adventure of reading and re-translation. Gradually the task became accomplished.

I should note that a number of other Tibetan commentaries to the *Seven Points for Training the Mind* have appeared in English translation in recent years. To the best of my knowledge, however, the present treatment by the First Dalai Lama is the most exhaustive. It is my hope that it may prove of value to Western students of Tibetan Buddhism, as well as to practitioners of the lojong tradition.

VI. A CONCLUDING OBSERVATION

The text of the First Dalai Lama that follows, *Training the Mind in the Great Way*, was written more than five hundred years ago. In turn it was written as a commentary to a spiritual legacy brought to Tibet more than four hundred years before that. Thus it is of considerable antiquity, and as a result it speaks in terms and symbols that are perhaps not always immediately accessible to the reader.

Yet its language contains a wonderful message to people of all ages. If we can look beyond the form to the essential content, its significance and relevance have not diminished with the centuries. On the contrary, our need for the spiritual qualities that it asks us to cultivate has only become more pronounced in the present age: qualities such as awareness of the fragility and preciousness of life, of the need to bring a basic sanity into our every action and to extend love and kindness to others. It suggests that these forces, coupled with the wisdom that mitigates our insatiable grasping, will make us into better, more harmonious human beings; and that through improving ourselves we will improve our life and, by extension, the world.

To hear the First Dalai Lama's message clearly we have to read his text as though he were speaking it to us. We have to open our hearts and minds, and suspend our imaginations. In thus reading we sit at the crossroads of two worlds: our own, and that of ancient Tibet.

The Tibetan symbol of the translator is the two-headed bird. This bird, it is said, is able to look behind itself to the land from where it came, and it can also look forward, to a new world. And as it is a single living being, it can interface these two realities.

To appreciate, enjoy and fully benefit from reading a text translated from a foreign culture we have to become like that two-headed bird, taking the images and symbols of a distant world and translating them into something relevant to our own lives and experience. Such is the task of the armchair philosopher and untraveled internationalist.

Undoubtedly it is a somewhat challenging endeavor, demanding considerable effort on the part of the reader. But those who make the effort know the rewards. They gain the ability to break the barriers of time; and they know no racial or cultural boundaries.

Glenn H. Mullin
Osel Ling Meditation Center
Missoula, Montana

Preamble

Homage to the spiritual masters,
Who are inseparable in nature
From the yidams, the meditational buddhas.

This tradition of "Training the Mind in the Great Way"[1] will be presented under three headings: an outline of the venerable source of the lineage, the greatness of the tradition, and the actual instructions.

I. THE VENERABLE SOURCE OF THE LINEAGE

The authentic source of the *lojong* lineage, which is stated in order to inspire in practitioners a healthy respect for the tradition, is none other than the illustrious Atisha himself. Atisha had received three lines of the lojong transmission: one from the (Indonesian) master Serlingpa (Tib., gSer-gling-pa), another from the (Indian) master Maitriyogi, and the third from his (Indian) guru Dharmarakshita.[2]

The tradition to be dealt with here is known as "The Essence of Nectar."[3] It is the oral tradition teaching for training the mind in the Great Way through the techniques of exchanging self-cherishing for the cherishing of others, and is the lojong

tradition that Atisha received from his teacher Serlingpa. This is stated in the root text,

**This essential, nectar-like oral teaching
Is the lineage coming from holy Serlingpa.**

That is to say, the lineage began with the Buddha and was passed down from generation to generation until eventually it came to the master Lama Serlingpa. Serlingpa passed the lineage to Atisha, who brought it to Tibet; and from him it was passed in various lines. I myself received four transmissions of these lojong teachings.

The first was from my precious root guru, the holy Lama Druppa Sherab[4] (Tib., Grub-pa-shes-rab); and the second was from Chennga Sonam Lhundrub (Tib., sPyen-snga-bsod-nams-lhun-grub-pa). Thirdly, from Lama Tukje Pawa (bLa-ma-thugs-rje-dpa'-ba) I received the lineage coming down from Sempa Chenpo Gyalsepa (Tib., Sems-pa-chen-po-rgyal-rses-pa). Fourthly, I received the transmission of the oral tradition coming down from the bodhisattva Lama Chekhawa (Byang-sems-'chad-kha-ba).[5]

This fourth lineage is based on the methods of transforming self-cherishing into a universal concern for all sentient beings, as taught in the chapter on meditation in (Shantideva's) *A Guide to the Bodhisattva Ways.*[6]

This lineage had come to Lama Tsongkhapa, the illustrious Je Rinpoche (Tib., bLa-ma-rje-rin-po-che). In the early days of Ganden Monastery[7] this illustrious master visited the Tiger's Peak in the Olkha mountains,[8] and while there passed these teachings to the Lama Namkha Paldenpa (Tib., bLa-ma-nam-mkha'-dpal-ldan-pa) of Ganden Jangtse Monastery[9] (Tib., dGa'-ldan-byang-rtse), from whom I myself later received them.

The tradition presented in this commentary is in accordance with the fourth of these lineages.

II. THE GREATNESS OF THE TRADITION

The excellence of the tradition is expressed in order to generate respect and inspiration within practitioners. Here the root text states,

Like a diamond, the sun and a medicinal tree:
Thus should this text and its essential points be
understood.

The first of the images given here is that of the diamond, and it is said that one should regard the words of this text as having the wondrous qualities of this extraordinary stone.

A diamond has four sides, and any piece of that diamond also has four sides, each of which reflects light with a beauty able to outshine the radiance of any ornament of ordinary gold. Moreover, a small fragment of this precious stone will still retain the name of "diamond," and will have the capacity to eradicate tremendous poverty.

Similarly, the practitioners who generate within their mindstream the essential wisdom embodied in a single passage of this instruction immediately outshine in greatness the qualities of (Hinayana adepts such as) *shravakas* or *pratyekabuddhas*.[10] They become known as bodhisattvas,[11] even if they are unable to perform the mighty bodhisattva deeds. The insight that they gain immediately begins to counteract the spiritual poverty of the world.

Secondly, one should understand the meaning of this text to be like the sun. A single ray of the sun's light has the power to eliminate the darkness of an entire continent, and its advent heralds full daybreak. In the same way, when realization of a fraction of this instruction is generated within the mindstream of a practitioner it brings with it the potency to eliminate the sickness of delusion and mental distortion, such as the negative habit of self-cherishing. The experience also heralds the advent of complete realization.

The words and meaning of the tradition should together be regarded as a medicinal tree. A medicine made from all parts of this tree has the ability to cure disease, and so does a medicine made from any specific parts of the tree. Similarly, this tradition as a whole shows the way to eliminate the illness of the deluded and distorted mind which is based on the self-cherishing syndrome, and also how to eliminate the illness created by the obscurations to highest knowledge. Any portion of this instruction has the same function. Integrating the tradition as a whole has this healing capacity, and so does integrating a specific aspect of the tradition.

III. THE ACTUAL INSTRUCTIONS

The actual instructions are given as seven points: the preliminaries; the actual body of the training, which is the instruction on how to develop the two types of *bodhichitta*, or enlightenment mind; transforming negative conditions into aids on the path to enlightenment; the doctrine of a practice for one lifetime; the signs of progress in the trainings; commitments of the tradition; and general advice to practitioners.

Point One: The Preliminaries

The first of the seven points in this tradition for training the mind in the Great Way is that of the preliminaries. Here the root text states,

First train in the preliminary practices.

This involves two phases: (I) the meditation of guruyoga, which is a method for establishing blessings on the mindstream; and (II) the methods for preparing oneself and making oneself into a vessel capable of undergoing the actual training.

I. THE MEDITATION OF GURUYOGA

The founder of our spiritual legacy, the mighty Buddha Shakyamuni,[12] first gave birth to the altruistic aspiration to achieve highest enlightenment in order to be of maximum benefit to all living beings. Then for three uncountable aeons he built up the stores of positive energy and wisdom. Finally at the Diamond Seat he achieved the complete perfection of omniscient buddhahood; and for the benefit of those to be trained he taught the eighty-four thousand aspects of the Dharma.

All of his teachings can be subsumed under two categories: those of the Hinayana, or Smaller Vehicle; and those of the Mahayana, or Great Vehicle.[13]

In the first of these vehicles he revealed the means of achieving nirvana, or liberation from cyclic existence, which is accomplished through transcending the belief in a truly existent self. Thus here the emphasis was on the methods of eliminating the I-holding ignorance, and very little was said about the methods of eliminating the self-cherishing attitude.

In the second category of teachings, those of the Mahayana, the Buddha mainly emphasized the methods for eliminating the self-cherishing attitude and replacing it with universal love and compassion. The goal here was to induce realization of the state of complete and perfect buddhahood as a means of benefiting all sentient beings.

To practice either of these vehicles successfully it is important to rely upon a qualified teacher. In particular, to accomplish the Mahayana methods it is important to train under a master accomplished in the Mahayana path.

Here it is said that the correct way to train under a spiritual master is to transcend the mind-set that sees the teacher as ordinary, and instead to learn to see him as an actual buddha.[14] Also, one must learn how to integrate his teaching.

There are numerous ways of conducting a guruyoga meditation session. A common method is to visualize that the guru sits in the space in front of you on a jeweled throne upheld by the eight lions of enlightenment. He is surrounded by all the lineage gurus, as well as by all the buddhas and bodhisattvas. These all dissolve into him, and he becomes an embodiment of all enlightened beings.

A second method is to imagine that he sits on a seat above your head. Sometimes here he is seen having a line of lineage gurus above him, with the Buddha at the top (to represent the successive generations in the line of transmission of the teachings). Alternately the lineage gurus, buddhas and bodhisattvas can be visualized as sitting in a circle around him.

At the crown, throat and heart of the guru are the syllables white *OM*, red *AH* and blue *HUM*, respectively.[15] Lights emanate forth from the blue *HUM*, summoning forth all lineage gurus, buddhas, bodhisattvas, shravakas, pratyekabuddhas, dharmapalas and guardians.

One makes offerings of the two waters and five sensory objects with the mantra *OM SARVA TATHAGATA ARGHAM PRATICCHA HUM SVAHA*[16] and so forth; and then as the mantric syllables *JAH HUM BAM HOH*[17] are said one visualizes that all invoked beings dissolve into the guru: the lineage gurus, buddhas and bodhisattvas into the upper half of his body; and the shravakas, pratyekabuddhas, dharmapalas and guardians into the lower half.

One can meditate in this way on gradually generating the vision of the guru as an embodiment of all holy beings; or one can simply reflect from the very beginning of the meditation session that the guru in fact already is this embodiment.

I will explain a simple meditation technique in accordance with the latter tradition. Above the crown of your head visualize a jeweled throne upheld by eight great lions. It is vast and extensive, and upon it is a meditation cushion made of a multicolored lotus with a moon disk. Seated there is your root guru in the form of Buddha Amitabha, his body red in color, his feet crossed in the vajra posture, his hands folded in his lap in the gesture of meditation. His body is adorned with all the major marks and minor signs of enlightenment; his speech is enriched with the sixty melodious qualities; and his mind possesses love, compassion, the enlightenment attitude and the wisdom that sees both the multiplicity and the final nature of all objects of knowledge. Smiling with joy, he looks on you with delight.

From the very beginning recollect that he is the embodiment of all gurus, all meditation deities, all buddhas and all dharmapalas. Then make offerings of the two purifying waters and five sensory objects with the mantras of *ARGHAM* and so forth, as explained earlier.

Next recite a verse of praise, such as the following:

Out of kindness the guru manifests in an instant
From the sphere of sublime great bliss.
O precious spiritual master, I pay homage
At the lotus beneath your vajra feet.

It is then appropriate to recite a seven-limbed offering and also the universal (mandala) offering. An excellent liturgy for the former of these is found in *The Aspiration of Samantabhadra*.[18] It reads as follows:

O lions amongst living beings,
Buddhas past, present and future,
To as many of you as exist in the ten directions
I bow with body, speech and mind.

On waves of strength of this king
Of praises of exalted, sublime ways,
With bodies numerous as atoms of the world
I bow to buddhas everywhere in space.

On every atom is found a buddha
Sitting amidst countless bodhisattvas.
To this infinite sphere of mystic beings
I gaze with eyes of faith.

With oceans of every possible sound
In eulogy of the perfect buddhas,
I give voice to their excellent qualities:
Hail those passed to bliss.

Garlands of flowers I offer them;
And beautiful sounds, supreme perfumes
Butter lamps and sacred incense
I offer to all awakened ones.

Excellent food, supreme fragrances
And a mound of powders as high as Meru
I arrange in mystic formation
And offer to those who have conquered
    themselves.

All these peerless offerings I hold up
In admiration for those gone to bliss.

In accord with exalted and sublime ways,
I prostrate and make offerings to the buddhas.

Long overpowered by attachment, anger and
  ignorance,
I have committed countless negative deeds
With acts of body, speech and mind.
Each and every one of these I now confess.

In the perfections of the buddhas and bodhisattvas
And the arhats in training and beyond,
And in the potential of every living being
I lift up my heart and rejoice.

O lights unto the ten directions,
Buddhas who have found the stage of
  enlightenment,
To all of you I offer this prayer:
Turn the incomparable wheel of Dharma.

Enter not into parinirvana
But work for the good of living beings.
For as many aeons as there are specks of dust
Stay with us and teach us, I pray.

By whatever small merits I may have amassed
By prostrating, making offerings,
Confessing, rejoicing and asking the buddhas
To remain and teach the Dharma,
All of it I dedicate now
To supreme and perfect enlightenment.

Then recite either the long or short universal (mandala) offerings. The short version is as follows:

A mandala base anointed with flowers, incense
  and scented water
And adorned with the King of Mountains,

The continents of the four directions,
And also the sun and the moon,
I offer to the field of enlightened ones.
May all beings enjoy this pure sphere.

Now focus attention on the visualization of your root guru, recollecting that he is an embodiment of all enlightened beings. Generate a sense of apprehension for the terrible sufferings found in cyclic existence, and engender the conviction that the spiritual master has the ability to guide you to the state beyond them. Contemplate that no matter what may befall you in future, be it happiness or difficulties, things high or things low, your great hope for liberation and enlightenment is none other than your own precious spiritual teacher.

Thinking like this recite the following words of refuge:

I take refuge in the guru, a precious buddha.
I take refuge in the Dharma master, a precious
    buddha.
I take refuge in the guru, who is Dharmakaya.
I take refuge in the guru, who is Sambhogakaya.
I take refuge in the guru, a supreme
    Nirmanakaya.

In this way generate a sense of refuge toward the guru, and not in mere words alone.

Then offer the following supplication to him:

O precious master, embodiment of all buddhas, I call to you. O precious master, source of the wonderful spiritual teachings, I call to you. O precious master, chief guide of all living beings in the three worlds, I call to you. O precious master, my source of refuge and hope, I call to you.

Inspire me to transcend every distorted state of mind. Inspire me to give birth to every clear state of mind. Inspire me to generate realization of the two types of bodhichitta. Bless my mindstream so that in this life, at death, in the intermediate state between death and rebirth, and also in all future lives the two bodhiminds may not become weak within me, but may always be manifest with ever-increasing power. Give me strength that I may take any difficulties and obstacles that arise as friends come to help me develop the two bodhiminds.

Offer this supplication many times from the very depths of your heart, until your eyes swim with tears, the hair on your body begins to tremble, and you are barely able to sit still. Then visualize that a stream of white light radiates forth from the crown of the guru's head. It comes to the crown of your head and flows down through your body, thus bestowing upon you waves of blessings of the guru's holy body and purifying all negative karmas collected in previous lives by means of physical action.

A stream of red light now shines forth from the guru's throat, coming to and dissolving into your throat. It bestows upon you waves of blessings of the guru's holy speech and purifies all negative karmas collected in previous lives by means of acts of speech.

Next a stream of blue light radiates forth from the guru's heart, coming to and dissolving into your heart. It bestows upon you waves of blessings of the guru's holy mind and purifies all negative karmas collected in previous lives by means of the mind.

Finally streams of white, red and blue lights radiate forth simultaneously from the guru's crown, throat and heart, coming to and dissolving into your crown, throat and heart. They bestow upon you every blessing and purify all negative karmic seeds, together with their instincts, collected in previous lives by means of the body, speech and mind.

Then repeat the stages of the above process beginning from the verse of refuge until the end of the supplication.

At the conclusion, visualize that the guru melts into a tiny ball of light. This light then descends into you, entering your body via the crown aperture and coming down to your heart.

Here it merges with your stream of consciousness.
Rest like this at length in single-pointed meditation on the inseparable nature of the guru and your own mind.

II. MAKING ONESELF INTO A VESSEL CAPABLE OF UNDERGOING THE TRAINING

This second preliminary practice involves four topics of contemplation: (A) the preciousness of a human life blessed with the eight freedoms and ten endowments; (B) death and impermanence; (C) the karmic laws of cause and effect; and (D) the unsatisfactory nature of cyclic existence.

A. THE PRECIOUSNESS OF HUMAN LIFE

The preciousness and rarity of a human life blessed with the eight freedoms and ten endowments is contemplated in four ways.

1. THE NATURE OF THE FREEDOMS AND ENDOWMENTS

This means that we have to recognize and appreciate just what constitutes the eight freedoms and ten endowments.

The eight freedoms refer to a rebirth in which the eight states of spiritual deprivation have been transcended. Four of these are given in reference to non-human states; the other four to human states.

The first three of the four non-human states of deprivation refer to being born by the forces of compulsive karma and delusion in any of the three lower realms, namely, the hell realms, the ghost realms and the realm of animals. The fourth deprivation is to be born from the forces of karma and delusion in any of the realms of the long-lived celestials, such as the worlds of the sensuous heavens, where the beings are distracted by an excess of sensory indulgence, or a celestial with no powers of discrimination, or in the heavens of form or formlessness.

As for the four deprivations of the human realm, this means to be born in an age when no buddha has come into the world; or although a buddha may have come, to take birth in a remote land where the four wheels of his teaching never reach;

or even though we take birth in a land where the enlightenment teachings have spread, we have serious physical or mental
handicaps, such as being born deaf or mute, or with incom-
plete mental faculties; or even if we are born in a central land
and have all faculties intact, we are held back because of being dominated by strong opinions contradicting spiritual
growth, such as failing to appreciate the karmic laws of cause
and effect.

These latter four are called states of deprivation because any
person born into them does not have the freedom to accomplish the practice of the holy Dharma. In the first three instances there is not the knowledge of what differentiates
Dharma from non-Dharma; and in the fourth there is simply
no inclination to cultivate spiritual knowledge.

As for the ten endowments, five of these are called 'personal'
and the other five 'environmental.' The five personal endowments are given (in a passage by Nagarjuna) as follows:[19]

Being born as a human, in a central land,
Having all sensory faculties intact,
Not having committed any of the terrible karmic deeds,
And having an inclination for the spiritual quest:
These are the five personal endowments.

That is to say, the five personal endowments are: (1) to have
taken birth as a human being; (2) to live in a central land, i.e.,
a place where the enlightenment teachings thrive; (3) to have
all the sense faculties, such as sight and hearing, etc.; (4) not
to have created any of the terrible karmic deeds, such as the
five inexpiable actions of killing one's mother, father, etc.; and
(5) having interest and conviction in the objects of spiritual
knowledge, such as the three baskets of scriptures, that explain the nature of the three higher trainings—discipline,
meditative absorption and wisdom.

These five are called 'personal endowments' because they
are conditions conducive to the practice of the spiritual path
and they are factors that are directly linked to one's personal
stream of being.

The second set are known as the five environmental endowments. They also are given in a verse (by Nagarjuna):

A buddha has come, the Dharma has been taught,
The teachings remain, practitioners exist,
And having the compassionate care of others:
These are the five environmental endowments.

That is to say, (1) a buddha has appeared in the world; (2) he has taught the holy Dharma; (3) his teachings and also (4) accomplished practitioners of his teachings still remain in the world; and (5) one experiences the compassionate care and support of spiritual friends in one's Dharma practice.

These five are called 'environmental endowments' because they are conditions conducive to Dharma practice and they are factors directly linked to phenomena other than one's own stream of being.

2. THEIR EXTRAORDINARY VALUE

The second topic to be contemplated is the extraordinary value of a human rebirth blessed by the eight freedoms and ten endowments.

This is explained in two contexts: its capacity to accomplish ultimate purposes, and its capacity to accomplish temporary purposes.

As for the first of these, a human rebirth blessed with the eight freedoms and ten endowments has the extraordinary value of being able to accomplish both the omniscient state of buddhahood and the state of final liberation, or nirvana.

The first of these attainments is achievable only by a human having the freedoms and endowments; no other life form is a suitable base for this attainment.

Concerning the second of the attainments, that of liberation, one must achieve at least the state of the path of insight (into emptiness) by relying on a human form. Only then, based on what one achieved with a precious human rebirth blessed with the freedoms and endowments, can one continue along the path in other life forms.

Snow Lion Publications

P.O. Box 6483
Ithaca, New York 14851

PLACE
POSTAGE
HERE

Snow Lion Publications

Our periodic mailings are an excellent way to learn of new publications as they are released. Please fill in your name and address below (or the name of an interested friend or book dealer). Just add postage and drop it in the mail. You'll be hearing from us......

Name _____

Street Address _____

City _____ State _____ Zip _____

The precious human rebirth is also very efficient in accomplishing temporary benefits. To be happy on the conventional level we require a healthy body, basic life necessities, good friends and other conducive conditions. The causes of acquiring these are living a disciplined lifestyle, cultivating a generous heart, practicing patience, and so forth. The best vehicle for internalizing these values is the precious human rebirth blessed by the freedoms and endowments.

3. THEIR RARITY

The third topic of contemplation is the rarity of acquiring a precious human rebirth blessed by the freedoms and endowments. We can appreciate the extreme rarity of this life form by contemplating both its causes and its nature.

The principal cause bringing about a precious human rebirth is cultivation of self-discipline, and this is something to which living beings rarely pay attention. Conversely, the cause of lower rebirth is lack of self-discipline and the consequent production of negative deeds, and these are things in which living beings almost constantly engage.

In the contemplation of rarity by nature, we should observe how few beings there are in the upper realms as compared to those in the lower. And even in the human world, over the course of history very few people indeed are blessed by all eight freedoms and ten endowments.

4. THE NEED TO EXTRACT THEIR ESSENCE

The fourth topic is the need for extracting the essence of our human life blessed by freedoms and endowments. At this time when we have achieved the very rare and meaningful human form having the eight freedoms and ten endowments we should exert ourselves to take its essence. The supreme essence to be extracted is the state of complete enlightenment, the attainment of perfect buddhahood.

In order to be inspired to extract the essence of our precious human life we must appreciate the nature of our spiritual situation. In particular, we should consider the following four facts.

The first of these is that we should make every effort to accomplish the spiritual path, for we all want to achieve happiness and avoid suffering; and the realization of these two goals depends upon our spiritual development.

The second is that we have the capacity to accomplish the spiritual path. We have the external condition of having met with spiritual masters, and we also have the internal condition of having a precious human rebirth blessed by the freedoms and endowments.

Thirdly we should begin our Dharma practice in this lifetime, and not procrastinate, for if we do not now achieve spiritual stability there is no guarantee that we will find a precious human rebirth again in the next.

Fourthly we should take up spiritual practice from this very moment, for it is uncertain just when death will come to us. We should think about death and impermanence, and contemplate how death certainly will come to us. There are serious disadvantages in living without mindfulness of death, and great benefits in cultivating this mindfulness.

Everyone intellectually understands that death will come one day. But most of us are dominated by the thought, "I won't die today, I won't die today." We have this sense right down to the very moment of our death.

The antidote to this deluded attitude is meditation on death and dying; and if we do not apply it our life becomes lost to the sphere of spiritual apathy and indulgence. As a result we give no attention to the accomplishment of inner values, nor to the attainments of liberation and enlightenment. Consequently we do not enter into the threefold path of hearing, contemplation and meditation, the means of accomplishing spiritual goals.

Without mindfulness of death and impermanence one's time easily is lost to the sphere of meaninglessness. Due to the overpowering forces of apathy and procrastination, this is often the case even if one seems to enter into spiritual practice. The deluded mind of attachment to the things of this life will continue to hold power over us and in turn induce us to enter into many negative and mistaken courses of action. The result will be the mere continuation of the samsaric syndrome of frustration and suffering.

Conversely, many beneficial effects arise from meditating on death and impermanence. Awareness of the transitory nature of all things becomes stable, and one will appreciate that this could be the last day of one's life. As a result the mind of attachment that grasps at the ephemeral things of this life is reversed, and one takes an increasing interest in things of lasting value, such as the creative energy generated by cultivating generosity, discipline, patience, enthusiasm, meditation and wisdom.

What exactly is the thought of death and impermanence upon which we should focus our meditation? It is not simply on the mind of fear that hopes to temporarily evade the sufferings of samsara, for until delusion and the distorted mind are transcended one will have to continue working within the samsaric environment.

Rather, one wants to become familiar with the thought of apprehension at meeting with death before significant progress on the spiritual path has been attained or at meeting with death before the causes of lower rebirth have been transcended and the causes of a rebirth conducive to enlightenment accomplished.

The methods for bringing about this transcendence and accomplishment can be practiced. There are great benefits in entering into this practice, and should one not do so there is every possibility that one will die with regret.

B. THE MEDITATIONS ON DEATH AND IMPERMANENCE

This involves three principal themes: (1) the certainty of death, (2) the uncertainty of the time of death, and (3) the fact that at death only spiritual wealth is of use to us. These are the three roots of the meditation, and each of them is supported by three reasonings.

1. THE CERTAINTY OF DEATH

The first root theme is the certainty of death. The three modes in which it is contemplated are as follows.

A) Meditate on how the Lord of Death comes to all living beings. No matter what the constitution of the body we have taken in this rebirth, it does not pass beyond the reach of death. No matter where we may live, it is not outside the territory of death. And no matter what the historical era, it is not a time free from death.

The first of these points (concerning the constitution of the body we have taken) is certainly true. If even the great accomplished spiritual beings of the past, like the sravakas, pratyekabuddhas, supreme nirmanakaya buddhas and so forth have shown the appearance of passing away, what need be said of ordinary mortals? As is pointed out in *The Collected Sayings of the Buddha*,[20]

> The perfect buddhas, the pratyekabuddhas, and also
> The shravakas who recorded the Buddha's teachings
> All passed away and left their bodies behind.
> What need to mention ordinary beings?

The second point (that no matter where we live we are still prone to death) is also certainly true. As *The Collected Sayings of the Buddha* puts it,

> The place where death does not reach
> Is a place that simply does not exist;
> There is no such place on earth, in the sky,
> In the depth of the ocean, nor on the mountain tops.

The third point (that the times make no difference) is also true. All beings of the past have died, and from this we can infer that all beings of the present and future will also do so. *The Collected Sayings of the Buddha* comments,

However many beings have come or will come,
All of them pass away to another world.
Therefore the wise understand impermanence
And abide in a firm practice of Dharma.

Death is steadily approaching, and nothing can turn it away: not speed, strength, wealth, magical substances, mantras nor medicines.

B) We should then contemplate how our life is constantly passing and there is no way of replenishing it. This is a sign that we will certainly die. Even if we have a natural lifespan of a hundred years, the passage of months quickly completes a year, the passage of days quickly completes a month, and days disappear with the passage of mornings and evenings, light and darkness.

C) Next we should contemplate how even now while we are alive we dedicate very little time to the pure practice of Dharma. Even if we were to live for a hundred years, in the final reckoning not much of this time would have been given to Dharma practice. Almost half of it will have been lost to sleep alone. Also, for the first ten years of our life, and also during the period after seventy years of age, we do not have much energy for spiritual endeavour. And in the time between these periods we have countless interruptions to practice, such as sorrow, suffering, an unhappy mind, illnesses, and so forth.

It is certain that we must die within a hundred years, but the day of our death is undetermined. It is not certain that we will die today, nor that we will not die today.

Thus it is best if we simply face death squarely, and think that this could be the last day of our life. When we take this attitude the mind naturally loses interest in ephemeral activities and looks to higher things, such as the ways of purification and spiritual openness.

2. THE UNCERTAINTY OF THE TIME OF DEATH

Meditation on the uncertainty of the time of death also involves three contemplations: *(A)* the lifespan in this world is not fixed, so the time of our death is unknown; *(B)* the conditions bringing death are numerous and causes supporting life few, thus making the time of our death uncertain; and *(C)* our physical body is very fragile and is easily destroyed.

A) There is no fixed lifespan in this world. Except for the legendary land of Draminyan, where lifespan is predetermined, in all other places it is of an unknown length. Especially here in the world of Dzambuling it is particularly unstable.[21]

In earlier aeons humans could live for unimaginable lengths of time; toward the end of the cosmic cycle the human lifespan will be as short as ten years. At no time is it of a fixed length.

B) The conditions for death are many and those for life are few. Moreover, any condition supporting life can easily become a condition bringing about our death.

The first of the above statements is certainly true. Sentient and insentient harms abound everywhere around us. There are countless malicious beings that could strike us down at any moment, such as violent and corrupt humans, vicious animals, various other types of non-humans, and so forth.

As for insentient dangers, there are external dangers from the four great elements, such as earthquakes and landslides, fires and floods, windstorms and other natural calamities. These can unleash themselves with an instant and deadly fury. Internally the elements of our body can fall out of balance and bring sudden death upon us.

C) Even the factors normally supportive of life can result in our death. Food and drink, so indispensable to our survival, can bring about our death through our eating too much or too little of it, or through its turning poisonous. Our house can collapse on us or bring about our death in a number of ways. Even our friends can deceive us and cause our premature death.

From the very moment of our birth we are constantly facing the possibility of instant death. In the end it becomes obvious that our body is fragile and is easily destroyed by the smallest circumstance.

3. AT THE TIME OF DEATH ONLY SPIRITUAL WEALTH IS OF VALUE TO US

Thirdly we should contemplate how at the time of death nothing but the forces of our spirituality are of any value to us. This also involves three themes.

A) At the time of death we may be surrounded by countless family members and friends, but we will have to go on alone into the hereafter.

B) We may own storehouses full of food and drink, but we will have to go on empty-handed. We may be dressed in the very finest of clothing, but we will have to enter the hereafter as naked as the day we entered this world.

C) Even this body that we so deeply cherish, with which we have been together since our very conception, will be separated from us. What need be said of other material possessions?

What will accompany us at the time of death? Only the seeds of the positive and negative karmas that we have cultivated during our lifetime. The seeds of negativity that follow us are potential causes of our harm, and have the capacity to bring us into states of great suffering.

At death our only assets are our spiritual knowledge and the seeds of positive karma that we have cultivated within ourselves. This spiritual knowledge then is our refuge and haven, our lord and protector, our guide and navigator.

Therefore from this very moment onward look to the ways that cultivate and strengthen spiritual knowledge.

C. THE KARMIC LAWS OF CAUSE AND EFFECT

The third topic of contemplation in making oneself into a vessel capable of undergoing the training is contemplating karma and its result. This is discussed under three headings: (1) the nature of karmic law, (2) in search of a spiritual refuge, and (3) purifying the mind of negative karma.

1. THE NATURE OF KARMIC LAW

There is no certainty when we shall die, but when death does come we will not simply transform into nothing. Nor do we have much reason to believe that we will enter into a state of liberation. As long as delusion and mental distortions are not transcended, we will continue to take rebirth in samsara.

The places of rebirth are basically of two types: there are the three higher realms, where beings mainly experience happiness, and the three lower realms, where they mainly experience suffering.

We should make it a daily exercise to reflect upon the nature of the lower realms. Ask yourself the question, "What would it be like if I were to take rebirth in one of the three realms of misery?"

Remember the advice of Acharya Nagarjuna:[22]

Every day think about the nature
Of the hot and the cold hells.
Think about the realm of the ghosts,
Who are tortured by hunger and thirst.
Look at and consider the predicament of the animals,
Who suffer greatly through lack of intelligence.

Contemplating these words daily gives rise to many beneficial effects. For example, the resultant knowledge of the nature of suffering causes our pride and arrogance to decrease, and we experience the thought that aspires to liberation. Also, through realizing the cause of suffering to be negative activity we experience the thought to transcend negativity.

Also, not wanting suffering and wanting to experience happiness, one experiences the thought to engage in creative activity, the cause of that happiness.

Furthermore, based on one's own experience of suffering and the inference of how other sentient beings also suffer, one experiences the thought of compassion for all beings.

Contemplation of the nature of karma and its fruit also leads to concern with the terrible miseries found in the various realms of samsara, and this in turn gives rise to a strong thought of turning for guidance to the Three Jewels of Refuge: the Buddhas, the Dharma and the Sangha.

A Guide to the Bodhisattva Ways[23] states,

Without suffering there is no yearning for freedom.
Therefore, mind, you should stand firm.

And also,

Moreover, suffering brings many benefits:
Experience of it eliminates one's arrogance,
Compassion arises for others who suffer in samsara,
And one comes to shun negativity and find joy in
    goodness.

The same text also states,

Who can afford me real protection
From the great terror of samsaric suffering?
With frightened eyes searching frantically
I look into the four directions for refuge.

Should I not find a refuge there,
I will be overcome by gloom.
Should I not find a refuge,
What then will I be able to do?

Therefore I now look for guidance
To the Buddhas who protect the world,
Who strive to shelter all that lives
And with great strength eradicate all fear.

Likewise I purely seek refuge
In the Dharma that the Buddhas have realized,
That dispels the terror of samsara;
And also I look to the assembly of bodhisattvas.

Trembling with concern I offer myself
To Samantabhadra, the Always Sublime Bodhisattva;
And to Manjushri, the Bodhisattva of Wisdom,
I turn with devotion and seek refuge.

Thus contemplating the nature of suffering is shown to have many beneficial effects.

What exactly are the sufferings of the lower realms? For the answer to this one should meditate upon the nature of life in the hells, the animal world, and the realm of the hungry ghosts.

A) Contemplating the Sufferings of the Hells

This involves three topics: *(1)* contemplating the sufferings of the hot hells; *(2)* contemplating the cold hells, and *(3)* contemplating the occasional hells.

(1) Contemplating the Sufferings of the Hot Hells

In general it is said that there are eight hot hells. The first of these is called 'Die and Revive.' Here, as a result of the forces of the karmic seeds of their previous actions, the beings constantly fight and harm one another with terrible weapons. They fall unconscious from the suffering of their wounds, but then a voice calls out to them from the skies and commands them to revive. They immediately come back to life and continue to suffer as before.

Below this, in the 'Black Line Hell,' dreadful torturers tie the beings down and draw black lines over their bodies. They then cut along these lines with saws, knives and hatchets.

In the 'Crushing Hell' one experiences being crushed between enormous mountains shaped like the heads of goats.

In the 'Pressing Hell' one is forced into an enormous metal machine and is slowly squashed, like sugarcane being pressed for its juices.

The beings born into the 'Gather and Crush Hell' are chased in herds. Eventually they are caught and are crushed beneath enormous boulders.

In the 'Hell of Shrieks' the beings are forced into iron houses blazing with fire. They cry out in anguish from the intense pain.

In the hell below this, called 'Loud Shrieks,' they escape into an outer chamber. But this also is made of iron and blazes with fire. The heat and suffering here is much more intense than before, and they cry out in loud shrieks.

For those born into the hell below this, called the 'Scorching Hell' the very surface of the earth seems to be made of red-hot metal. Guards torture their victims with flaming spears, impaling them from the anus through to the crown of the head. Fire shoots out of all bodily apertures.

Below this, in the 'Super Scorcher Hell,' the guards pierce the bodies of their victims with three-pointed spears of red-hot iron. The points protrude from the shoulders and crown of the head. Again, fire shoots out of all apertures. The beings here are also boiled in molten iron until all skin and flesh falls away and only the skeleton is left; they are then taken out and revived, and the process is repeated.

Finally in Avicchi, the 'Hell Without Respite,' fire blazes from all directions. Here it is so hot that the flames are indistinguishable from one's body. The only sound heard is the terrible roar of raging flame.

How long do the beings born into these hells have to stay there? Imagine a great kingly celestial being who lives for five hundred years, and that a single day in the life of this being is equal in length to fifty human years. Calculate in this way for thirty of those days in a month, twelve months in a year, and so on for five hundred years.

One day in the least of these hells, 'Die and Revive,' is equal in duration to the complete lifespan of that kingly celestial. Thirty of those days make a month; twelve of those months make a year; and so on for five hundred such years.

Each hell below this doubles in duration. The 'Super Scorcher Hell' continues for half an intermediate aeon; and Avicchi, the 'Hell Without Respite,' for a full intermediate aeon.

Should the sufferings of these hot hells fall upon you, you would find them extremely difficult to bear; for they are exceedingly long and intense. At the moment we find it difficult to endure the pain of placing our hand in hot coals for just a short while; so what can be said of our ability to endure the pain of the hot hells?

Of all the sufferings in samsara those of the hot hells are the most terrible, and especially those of Avicchi, the 'Hell Without Respite.' As (Arya Nagarjuna's) *A Letter to a Friend* puts it,

Of all pleasures, that free from clinging
Is said to be the greatest. So too
Of all the forms of suffering in samsara
The suffering of Avicchi Hell is greatest.

Being struck continuously for a day
By three hundred terrible spears
Is a small suffering compared to that of the hells.
No image can convey the experience.

We can have no certainty that we ourselves will not be re-born in these hells. Their cause is negative and harmful activity of an intense degree, and even now it seems that our body, speech and mind create much of this. Moreover, we have been doing so in countless previous lifetimes since time without beginning.

The karmic seeds of these negativities lie within our mindstream, and they will continue to do so until either removed by application of the spiritual antidotes or else ripened upon us as the experience of suffering. Until they have all been transcended we remain prone to such a lower rebirth.

On the four sides of each of the eight hells are pits of red-hot coals. When one tries to escape through them one sinks in up to one's knees. As one's legs enter the coals the flesh and bones burn away, yet when one pulls the legs back out they become restored.

Next to this hell one encounters a swamp full of corpses. When one attempts to cross it one sinks in up to the waist. Worms having a white head, black body and a mouth with very sharp teeth attack and chew holes through one's flesh to the very marrow.

One then comes to the Highway of Razors Hell. One attempts to escape down the highway; but it is made of sharp razor blades, and as one runs along the road the blades cut into one's feet and legs. The legs are restored, and the process continues.

Next one arrives at the Forest of Sword-like Leaves. The leaves fall off the trees as one runs below, gouging terrible wounds into one's body.

You are then chased and bitten by dogs with iron jaws, and attempt to climb into the trees to escape. The thorns of the trees turn their sharp points downward and pierce you viciously. Crows with iron beaks attack from above and peck at your face and eyes. You try to descend, but now the thorns turn their points upward and again rip at your flesh.

Finally you come to the River of Ashes. You attempt to cross it, but once you have entered you become tossed up and down like rice being rapidly boiled in a large pot. You try to escape, but your exit becomes blocked by sinister guards bearing weapons.

(2) Contemplating the Sufferings of the Cold Hells
It is said that there are eight of these, and that they are located in the cold darkness under the earth, far to the north of the hot hells.

In the 'Hell of Blisters' the bodies of the inhabitants break out in terrible blisters due to the intense cold.

In the hells below this the bodies of the inhabitants break out in enormous blisters that burst and ooze with pus. The beings cry out with the pain of coldness; and they wail. Their bodies turn blue with cold; and they crack open into five pieces, like a blue utpala flower. In the hell below this, 'Cracking Like a Lotus,' the bodies turn red and crack into eight pieces, like a lotus; and in 'Cracking Like a Great Lotus' the bodies of the inhabitants crack into hundreds or even thousands of pieces, exposing their inner organs, such as lungs and heart, to the intense cold. Such are the sufferings that they must experience.

How long do these sufferings continue? If we were to have a large container full of eighty measures of sesame seeds, and if we were to remove one seed every hundred years, the time taken to remove all the seeds is equal to the lifespan in the shortest of these, the 'Hell of Blisters.'

Each of the hells below is twenty times in duration the one above it, for each of the eight; thus it becomes twenty times twenty times twenty, and so forth.

Should these intense and prolonged sufferings fall upon you,

you would find them difficult indeed to bear. For example, at the moment we can hardly bear the suffering of staying outside in the ice and snow for merely a single day. What then can be said of our ability to endure the sufferings of the cold hells!

However, we can have no confidence that we will not take rebirth there. In the the past we have generated plenty of negative karma, have stolen from and belittled holy objects, and have lived by views conflicting with the spiritual path. Even now we do these things; and in the many past lives we've experienced since beginningless time we have undoubtedly accumulated countless such negative karmic seeds.

(3) Contemplating the Sufferings of the Occasional Hells
The occasional hells are said to be located near the hot and cold hells. They are in rivers, deserts, mountains and so forth. Their specific places, and also the length of the lifespans in them, is not predetermined.

As for the sufferings experienced in them, this can be read in other scriptures.

B) Contemplating the Suffering of the Animal Realms

Some animals live in the great oceans, and here they are as thick as flies collecting on discarded alcohol makings. From there they evolve into the worlds of humans and celestials.

What are their sufferings like? Sometimes the large ones eat the small; and in other instances many small ones work together to kill and eat the large. Many are raised and then killed by man: some for their wool, and others for their pearls, bones, flesh or skins. Still others are exploited for work, being punched and kicked, or struck with sticks, whips and iron hooks. They must carry heavy loads for their owners, and are pulled along by ropes tied to a nose ring. Others are hunted, trapped and killed by man.

How long do the animals live? In general it is said that they have no fixed lifespan, although the longest-lived is said to survive for an intermediate aeon.

If the suffering of the animal realms were to fall on us today, we would indeed find it difficult to bear. At the moment we seem to find it hard to endure even the sting of a tiny insect. Unfortunately we can have no confidence of not being reborn there in some future life. The cause of such a rebirth is negative and harmful activity of an intermediate intensity; and even now we seem to create these almost continuously with acts of body, speech and mind. Moreover, we have been doing so for countless previous lives since time without beginning.

C) Contemplating the Sufferings of the Ghost Realms

The restless ghosts are said to live in a world five hundred *yojanas*[24] beneath the earth. Those who appear in the human and celestial realms are said to proceed from there.

There are thirty-six main types of restless ghosts, but these are usually subsumed into three basic groups: those with outer obscurations, those with inner obscurations, and those with obscurations upon obscurations.

The ghosts with outer obscurations see rivers and lakes; but when they rush toward them to drink they are fought away by guardians holding swords and spears. Or else the water of the river or lake turns into pus and blood for them and they are unable to approach it.

Those with inner obscurations have a mouth the size of the eye of a needle, and a stomach as large as Mount Meru. Thus even though they have no external hindrance to their acquiring food and drink, they are never able to do so and thus are unable ever to satisfy their hunger and thirst.

Those with obscurations upon obscurations suffer in a variety of ways.

For some, whenever they eat or drink anything it bursts into flame and scorches them. Others can ingest only filthy substances like excrement and urine, and are unable to consume normal foods. Still others cannot find even filth to sustain themselves.

Some can eat and drink only their own flesh and blood, and are unable to consume anything else, while others are burned by the cool moonlight in summer and find the warm winter sun excruciatingly cold.

There are some types that see fruit orchards or rivers, but when they rush toward them the fruit or the water disappears. These and many other sufferings of the ghost realms have been described in detail in (Arya Nagarjuna's) *A Letter to a Friend.*

How long does their life continue? It is said that a month in human time is a day in their life; thirty such days make a month, and twelve such months make a year. They live for five hundred such years.

Should the suffering of the ghost realm come to us, we would find it difficult indeed to bear. At the moment we find it hard to take the challenge of going without food for a mere five or six days. What then can we say of the ghost sufferings?

However, we can have no confidence that we will not be re-born there. The cause of such a rebirth is the accumulation of negative karmic seeds of mild intensity, and also the seeds of miserliness and attachment. We have collected many such seeds in this lifetime alone, not to mention in all the previous lives we've experienced since beginningless time.

This is the nature of the sufferings of the three lower realms of samsara. Make every effort to abandon the cause of being reborn in them, which is the collection of negative karma. And strive instead for the cause of higher rebirth, which is the collection of positive karma and goodness.

Moreover, the supreme goodness is the two bodhichittas, or enlightenment minds, so apply yourself diligently to cultivating and achieving them.

It is uncertain how much time we have left in this life. We would be wise immediately to develop a healthy concern with the nature of the lower realms, to turn for guidance to the Three Jewels of Refuge—the Buddhas, the Dharma and the Sangha—and, in order for our spiritual search to remain pure, to develop clear understanding of the workings of the karmic laws of cause and effect.

2. IN SEARCH OF SPIRITUAL REFUGE

Generally it is said that the door by which one enters into Buddhist practice, and thus the gateway of the path leading to enlightenment, is the act of turning for refuge to the Buddhas, the Dharma and the Sangha. Thus it is an undertaking of considerable importance.

Traditionally the subject of refuge is taught under four headings: *(A)* the psychological basis for taking refuge, *(B)* the objects which are the focus of refuge, *(C)* the context of refuge, and *(D)* advice for those who have taken refuge.

A) The Psychological Basis for Taking Refuge

Two psychological factors should be present in order for a person to be inspired to take refuge. The first of these is a realistic awareness of the dangers inherent in imperfect samsara. The second is the knowledge that the Buddhas, the Dharma and the Sangha have the ability to bring about spiritual benefits that can be of great value to you in the effort to transcend these dangers and can enable you to rise above all fear.

B) The Objects Which Are the Focus of Refuge

What kind of an object can serve as an effective focus of refuge? Here *The Hundred and Fifty Praises*[25] states,

To those who have utterly transcended
Every fault and shortcoming
And have cultivated to final perfection
Every quality of spiritual excellence,
It is quite appropriate for someone with wisdom
To honor and show them the highest respect
And to dwell within their teachings.

In other words it is the fully enlightened beings, the buddhas who have transcended all faults and who possess every excellence, to whom one should turn for guidance.

Why are the fully enlightened beings a worthy object of refuge? Because they themselves have achieved liberation from every samsaric fear, and also they have the wise and skillful means for guiding others beyond the states of fear. In addition, they are motivated solely by love and compassion, and they seek to benefit all sentient beings without holding the slightest partiality for some over others.

This is not the case with the worldly gods, such as Ishvara. They themselves are not beyond samsaric faults, such as jealousy; nor do they have all the means of liberation at their disposal, for they themselves have not yet achieved final liberation; nor are they motivated solely by impartial, universal love and compassion.

Because the enlightened beings are worthy and effective objects of refuge it follows that the Dharma, their teachings, is also a worthy refuge object. Similarly the sangha, who are the advanced practitioners of their teachings, must also be worthy.

C) The Context of Refuge

The tradition of taking refuge involves four topics: *(1)* appreciating the excellence of the refuge objects; *(2)* appreciating their uniqueness; *(3)* the refuge perspective; and *(4)* not mistaking the refuge objects.

(1) Appreciating the Excellence of the Three Jewels

Appreciating excellence means that one takes refuge within the sphere of knowing the extraordinary qualities of each of the Three Jewels: the buddhas, the Dharma, and the sangha.

The excellence of the buddhas is discussed in terms of the wondrous nature of their body, speech, mind and enlightened activity.

The extraordinary nature of the physical manifestations of the enlightened beings is described in *A Tapestry of Verse*,[26]

> The physical manifestations of an enlightened being
> Are delightful to behold, and are healing to the eye,
> Like a beautiful constellation of stars
> Radiant in a cloudless autumn sky.

The speech of an enlightened being is such that the things he says are heard by the different listeners in direct response to the spiritual questions that they have on their minds at the time.

It is said that if all sentient beings were simultaneously to ask a question of an enlightened being he would comprehend all those inquiries in a single moment; and although only one answer would be given, all the various beings would hear it in their own language in a manner that seemed to directly address their personal, individual concerns.[27]

The Chapter of the Truthful One[28] states,

> Should all the sentient beings that exist
> Simultaneously ask pointed questions,
> A buddha would understand them all
> In a single moment of thought
> And answer all with one melodious reply.

The subject of the qualities of a buddha's mind is taught in two parts: the qualities of knowledge and the qualities of compassion.

It is said that a buddha directly knows all objects of knowledge as clearly as a piece of transparent fruit held in the palm of the hand.

A buddha's wisdom pervades all objects of knowledge. For others, the objects of knowledge are simply too vast, and their wisdom too small. *In Praise of the Praiseworthy*[29] puts it this way:

> The wisdom of only a fully enlightened being
> Pervades all objects of knowledge.
> For beings on lower spiritual stages
> This wisdom still remains to be known.

Ordinary sentient beings are driven solely by delusion and the distorted mind. The fully enlightened buddhas, on the other hand, are driven solely by compassion. They dwell in an unbroken stream of love and compassion for all living beings. *The Hundred and Fifty Praises* states,

> All of the unenlightened sentient beings
> Without exception are bound in delusion.
> But a buddha has long been supported by compassion
> And by the thought to liberate beings from delusion.

Thus should I first pay homage to the buddhas?
Or should it be directed at the great compassion
That inspires them to remain in samsara
And to work tirelessly to liberate living beings?

As for the enlightened activity of a fully accomplished buddha, it is said that the magical feats of his/her body, speech and mind arise spontaneously and in an unbroken stream in order to benefit the sentient beings of the world.

From the side of the sentient beings, they are in need of guidance and assistance. As for the buddhas, there is no perfection with which they are not endowed, and there are no living beings in a state of imperfection so low that the buddhas cannot bring them guidance.

In brief, the buddhas do everything possible to bring goodness, enlightenment and joy into the world, and to eliminate negativity, ignorance and suffering from within the mindstreams of the living beings.

The excellence of the Dharma. The extraordinary quality of the jewel of Dharma is that through the practice of it one accomplishes the state of complete and perfect enlightenment.

If we can appreciate the greatness of the buddhas then we should be able to appreciate the greatness of the Dharma; for the buddhas who possess every excellence achieved their state of perfection by first listening to the Dharma teachings and then internalizing the meanings through applying the instructions and meditating on the path.

The excellence of the sangha. If we can appreciate the excellence of the Dharma we should also be able to appreciate the excellence of the sangha; for the sangha are beings who have achieved high spiritual states through the study and practice of the Dharma.

(2) Appreciating the Individual Uniqueness of the Three Jewels
The individual uniqueness of the character of the Three Jewels is that the buddhas represent the state of complete and perfect enlightenment; the Dharma is the product of that enlightenment; and the sangha are the practitioners who apply them-

selves correctly to the Dharma.

The individual uniqueness of their enlightening activity is that the buddhas transmit the Dharma; the Dharma brings transcendence from delusion and suffering; and the sangha inspire practitioners in their efforts to realize the Dharma.

The individual uniqueness of how they should be perceived is that the buddhas are to be honored; the Dharma is to be realized; and the sangha are to be regarded as those with whom it is meaningful to associate.

The individual uniqueness of how they should be cultivated is that the buddhas are to be respected and honored; the Dharma is the yoga to be integrated; and the sangha are those with whom one should share spiritual and social joys.

As for the individual uniqueness of how they are to be practiced as mindfulness meditations, firstly mindfulness of the buddhas is given in the passage,

> A buddha is a bhagawan, a tathagata, an arhat, and a fully enlightened one. He is one endowed with knowledge and its foundation, a sugata, a knower of the world, an unsurpassed teacher for those to be trained, a leader of humans and celestial beings.

Mindfulness of Dharma is similarly stated,

> The Dharma of a bhagawan is elegantly spoken, perfectly perceived, free of all faults, enduring, well conveyed, meaningful to behold, and an object to be realized by the wise through personal experience.

And again for the sangha,

> The sangha, those who heed the words of the enlightened ones, are excellent in their mode of being, precise in their mode of being, and gracious in their mode of being.

The individual uniqueness of how the Three Jewels amplify the force of one's merit is that a supreme increase occurs respectively (for the three): in regard to a single being, in regard to the Dharma, and in regard to the community of beings.

(3) The Refuge Perspective

The refuge perspective is that one turns to the buddhas as being the source that reveals the path of refuge, one turns to the Dharma as being the actual object of refuge, and one turns to the sangha as being the friends supporting the practice of refuge.

(4) Not Mistaking the Refuge Objects

Not mistaking the refuge objects means that one should have a mature and well-reasoned awareness of the qualities that differentiate the Buddhist from the non-Buddhist traditions, and on the basis of that knowledge should feel a stronger karmic connection with the Buddhist path.

In general one should have a sense of the buddhas as completely enlightened beings who have abandoned all imperfections and achieved all realizations, and that sense should be lacking concerning lesser masters.

As is said in *In Praise of the Superior Ones*,[30]

I give up on ordinary spiritual teachers
And turn for refuge to the Enlightened Ones.
And if you ask why I do so,
It is because the Enlightened Ones
Have no imperfections but have every excellence.

The same text elsewhere states,

The more I read, contemplate and reflect upon
The writings of ordinary spiritual teachers,
The more my mind develops confidence
In the way pointed out by the Enlightened Ones.

In brief, the Buddhist way is a joyous path that produces a joyous result. This cannot be said for many other so-called spiritual disciplines.

These qualities of the buddhas and the enlightenment path that they taught will naturally carry over to the sangha, the practitioners of that path.

D) Advice for Those Who Have Taken Refuge

This will be presented under two outlines: *(1)* the advice as found in *The Summary;*[31] and *(2)* the advice generally given in the oral tradition.

(1) Advice from The Summary

The Summary lists two sets of four pieces of advice. The first set is comprised of the following four factors: to rely upon the holy beings; to listen to the holy Dharma; to consider the Dharma well; and to practice according to the teachings. That is to say, having turned to the buddhas for guidance one should understand the spiritual master to be the root of the enlightenment path and then cultivate an effective working relationship with him/her.

Refuge in the buddhas means that one takes the teacher of the path as the source of guidance. The practice that synchronizes is the practice that regards the teacher of the path as the model.

As for the second and third factors: Having taken refuge in the Dharma one should consider well the teachings given by the buddhas and their advanced disciples. Refuge in the Dharma means that one should regard the scriptural and insight transmissions of Dharma as the objects to be realized. The practice that synchronizes is to listen well to the Dharma and to take it as one's guideline in practice.

The fourth factor is explained as follows. Having taken refuge in the sangha one should cultivate the path and cultivate what is harmonious with it. Refuge in the sangha means that one should regard the sangha as friends in the practice of the path. Thus practicing in synchronicity means that in practicing the path one takes the sangha as one's model.

The second set of four is as follows: not falling into sensory distraction; adopting the trainings purely; showing compassion to sentient beings; and delighting the Three Jewels at all times.

Concerning the first of these, the meaning is that one should appreciate the shortcomings of constantly allowing the mind to chase after external objects, and should divert it from doing so.

The second factor is that one should take up the trainings with the stablizing force of the precepts prescribed by the Buddha.

As for the third factor, the buddhist doctrine was revealed because of the compassion that the enlightened masters have for all living beings. Therefore practitioners of that doctrine should try to regard all living beings with compassion, and should refrain from harming them in any way.

The fourth factor advises that we should make daily offerings to the Three Jewels.

(2) Advice Given in the Oral Tradition
This is of two kinds: individual advice and general advice.

The individual advice is also of two kinds: that concerning what is to be cultivated; and that concerning what is to be abandoned.

The advice concerning what is to be cultivated is in harmony with what is said in *The Sutra of Buddha's Passing*.[32] Here three pieces of advice are given, one for each of the Three Jewels.

The first is that once one has taken refuge in the buddhas one should no longer worship worldly spirits. If this is the case with the powerful worldly celestials such as Vishnu and the like, what then can be said for mundane nature spirits and ghosts!

Here it should be noted that although it is not appropriate to rely upon worldly deities for ultimate purposes and in such a way that one's refuge in the buddhas is belittled, it is acceptable to propitiate them for conventional matters, such as assisting in bringing about conditions conducive to one's practice and realization of the Dharma.

Secondly, the observance to be cultivated by those who have taken refuge in the Dharma is always to regard other sentient beings with love and compassion. This entails refraining from binding or beating them, putting them in small pens or cages, putting rings through their noses, forcing them to carry excessively heavy loads, and so forth.

Thirdly, it is said that one should not spend too much time with those of extreme views. In other words, someone who has taken refuge in the sangha should not allow him/herself to become adversely influenced by obsessive people who constantly generate negative energy toward the Three Jewels and the practice of the enlightenment path.

The advice concerning what is to be avoided is also threefold, again there being one for each of the Three Jewels. The first of these is that someone who has taken refuge in the buddhas should refrain from belittling physical representations of the enlightened beings, such as statues, paintings, and so forth, regardless of their artistic merit. Avoid treating them with disrespect, such as by criticizing them, using them as objects of collateral, and so forth. Instead, look upon them with respect, as though they were the actual Buddha himself. *A Letter to a Friend* states,

No matter what the quality of an image of the sugatas,
It should be seen as an object of devotion,
Even if made out of the simplest wood.

Thus one should not belittle the holy images by making negative comments such as, "This image of the Buddha is like this or that," or, "This image is too large and is made from too much expensive material. It should never have been made."

The karmic importance of transcending negativity toward the Three Jewels is illustrated by the following anecdotes.

A man once heavily ridiculed some members of the sangha, saying things like, "You with the head of an elephant, what do you know about Dharma or non-Dharma!" In this way he insulted various sangha members by saying that they had heads shaped like those of eighteen different animals. It is said that as a result he was reborn as a sea monster with eighteen heads, each one the shape of a different animal.

Also, long ago after the parinirvana of Buddha Krakuch-chanda (i.e., the first buddha of this age, of which the histori-cal Buddha Shakyamuni was the fourth), a king commissioned the construction of a large stupa to enshrine this holy being's remains. One of the craftsmen complained twice, saying, "It is impossible to create such an enormous monument." Later, when the stupa's construction was complete he had a change of heart and offered a golden bell to it. It is said that as a re-sult he was reborn as a dwarf who was both ugly and exceed-ingly short, but who had a wonderfully melodious voice.

Here the advice related to refuge in the Dharma is that one should not underestimate a single line of the teachings. One should not regard holy books as objects of collateral or busi-ness, nor place scriptures on the bare earth. Nor should one use them as pillows, nor pack them in cases containing mun-dane items such as shoes, etc. The scriptures should be seen as being embodiments of the actual enlightenment methods.

Thirdly, the advice for those who have taken refuge in the sangha is to abandon all unworthy and negative attitudes to-ward the ordained community, such as by thinking, "This person does not live up to the robes," or "These monks or nuns are not of my sect, so there is no need to respect them," and so forth.

Look upon all sangha members as though they were highly accomplished beings with insight into the meaning of final reality.

The karmic effect of showing respect to the Three Jewels is that one will come to be treated with respect oneself. *The King of Absorptions Sutra*[33] states,

> Based upon the deed that was done,
> One receives a commensurate result.

The general advice of refuge is given in six general instructions.

(i) From the beginning one's refuge should be inspired by an appreciation of the uniqueness and excellence of the Three Jewels, and should be supported by repeated contemplation of the refuge objects. It should be based upon an informed awareness of the difference between the buddhist and non-buddhist paths, and should understand the individual qualities and special natures that differentiate each of the Three Jewels from one another.

(ii) One should contemplate the beneficial effects of the Three Jewels of Refuge and constantly exert oneself at making offerings to them. For example, offer a small portion of the first and best portion of each meal that you take. Whenever any happiness or pleasure arises, interpret it as being a product of the kindness of the Three Jewels and offer devotions.

These offerings of devotion are discussed in relation to two issues: the act of making offerings and the thought behind the offering.

The first of these, the act of offering, is discussed from ten perspectives. Firstly there is the offering made to a manifestation of the buddhas. By this is meant the act of focusing one's devotion upon a specific embodiment of the buddhas.

Then there is the offering made to a stupa; that is to say, focusing one's devotion upon a monument containing relics of a buddha.

The third is the direct offering. It is an actual offering placed in front of an actual image of a buddha or stupa.

The fourth is the indirect offering. Here no actual image of a buddha or a stupa is present. Rather, one visualizes these images and then sends forth offerings to them.

It should be pointed out that when one makes these offerings to an actual image of a buddha or stupa one should do so in the awareness that the image serving as the object of the offering is in fact identical to the nature of all such images. That is to say, one makes offerings to a single image of the Buddha or a stupa containing relics of him, but one imagines that the offering goes out to all buddhas of the three times and to all stupas of the ten directions. This gives rise to an unprecedented wave of meritorious energy.

The next advice is to perform the offering ritual oneself. This means that one does not, out of apathy, laziness or unconscientiousness, have others perform the offering in one's stead. Rather, one places the objects being offered on the altar oneself with one's own two hands.

The sixth is to have someone else make offerings in one's stead. Here one is moved by compassion on seeing a person impoverished and in a state of suffering, and thinks to oneself, "If I can help this person to increase his store of positive karmic energy by making offerings to the Three Jewels it will lead him to happiness." However, one should also participate in the process directly with one's own hands. This causes the meritorious energy to become especially sublime.

Next is the offering of things. This includes objects such as flowers, incense, butterlamps, scented water, foods, music, cloth, ornaments, and so forth.

The eighth is the vast offering. This refers to the duration of the offering process, the quality and quantity of the materials, whether manifest or unmanifest, the strength of the mental attitude, and so forth.

The root of virtue of having made the offering should be dedicated to peerless enlightenment.

Next is the offering free from the delusions. This means that, without falling under the influence of delusions such as apathy, laziness, mindlessness, and so forth, one makes offerings with one's own hands; one encourages others to do so; one does so with intense conviction; one does so without allowing the mind to wander in unconducive directions; one does so without falling under the influence of the delusions; one does so without hoping that one will receive something material in return; and one only offers appropriate things.

And just what is inappropriate? This includes things like the types of incense used for exorcism and the removal of evil spirits, etc., the (poisonous) flower *Gynandropsis pentaphylla*, and objects that are poisonous, harmful or repugnant.

As for the offering of actual things, if one is not able to prepare these oneself nor to obtain them from others, it is sufficient just to rejoice in offerings of this nature made by all the buddhas of the three times.

One can also offer (or visualize offering) unowned things, such as wild flowers and fruit, forests of trees, pure water, the jewels and precious gems that lie undiscovered under the earth and in the oceans, and so forth.

The tenth is the offering of practice. This includes trainings such as meditation upon the four immeasurable attitudes and upon the four seals of Dharma; dwelling in mindfulness of the Three Jewels and the transcendental perfections; meditating upon voidness; meditating upon the thirty-seven wings of enlightenment; cultivating the transcendental perfections; meditating upon the four ways of benefiting trainees; and so forth.

As for the thought behind the offering, this is explained as follows. When one makes offerings to the Three Jewels in accordance with the ten outlines given above one should think, "Immeasurable meritorious energy arises from making just a small offering." The condition giving rise to that is the presence (of the Jewels of Refuge), a peerless field of excellence, a peerless field of benefit.

Also there is the focus of the offering, the buddhas, supreme of all living beings; jewels appearing in this world as rarely as does the *udumvara* flower; unmatched, for only one buddha with the destiny to serve as a universal teacher appears in the three thousand world systems at a time; the support of everything good in the world and beyond.

It is important to include mindfulness of refuge in our daily activities. For example, eating and drinking are activities that we enjoy every day. Hence offering a small portion of every meal to the Three Jewels is an easy and simple method of increasing our store of meritorious karma. Therefore make offerings by sending forth to the Three Jewels a small portion of whatever you enjoy.

(iii) Thirdly, one should dwell within meditative recollection of great compassion, and encourage others in the tasks of refuge.

(iv) In all of one's works and for all needs one should turn to the Three Jewels of Refuge, make offerings to them, and then send forth a prayer. Success will certainly follow. If instead of this we turn to the worldly gods in times of need, which is what non-Buddhists do, success is not so probable an outcome.

(v) Fifthly, we should remain aware of the beneficial effects of maintaining refuge, and from within that sphere of appreci-

ation should recite the refuge formula three times each day and three times each night. Thus it is important to know the beneficial effects of refuge. These are described in two ways: the manner in which they are presented in *The Summary*, and the presentation found in the oral tradition.

The Summary gives two sets of four benefits of refuge. The four beneficial effects in the first set are: one will gain a vast store of meritorious energy; one will attain joy and supreme happiness; one will achieve extraordinary levels of meditation; and one will attain extraordinary wisdom.

The Dharani of the Immortal Drumbeat[34] states,

> The accomplished buddhas are inconceivable,
> The holy Dharma is inconceivable,
> The exalted sangha is inconceivable,
> Their beneficial effects are inconceivable.

Also *The Condensed Perfection of Wisdom Sutra*[35] states,

> If the meritorious energy of taking refuge
> Were to assume physical form,
> The 3,000 world systems would be too small a vessel.
> How can you measure the waters of a vast ocean
> By scooping with mere tiny handfuls?

And from *The Sayings on Mindfulness*,[36]

> If any person thrice daily and nightly
> Practices mindfulness of the buddhas
> And takes refuge in the buddhas,
> They will achieve rebirth as a human.

These same images can equally be applied to refuge in the Dharma and also the sangha. By contemplating these many beneficial effects, one experiences joy and supreme happiness.

As for the third and fourth factors, these are explained as follows. With the thought of spiritual stability one turns for guidance and inspiration to the Three Jewels. Based on this stability one achieves the training in discipline; and in turn on that foundation one goes on to achieve the training in meditative absorption. With discipline and meditation as one's supports, one easily achieves the training in wisdom. Then subsequently with the attainment of wisdom one achieves the state of spiritual liberation.

The second set of four beneficial effects arising from refuge is as follows: one gains great protection; the previously developed spiritual obscurations, which give rise to unwanted sufferings, become purified; one is placed in the company of holy beings; and one delights all enlightened and exalted beings.

As for the beneficial effects of refuge as mentioned in the oral tradition, these are eightfold. The first is that one becomes a member of the Buddhist community. A Buddhist by definition is someone who looks to the buddhas as the teachers, the Dharma as the actual source of liberation and enlightenment, and the sangha as friends who help on the way. Conversely if we have not developed a firm sense of refuge we are not a Buddhist, no matter what other spiritual disciplines we might cultivate.

The second beneficial effect is that one becomes a suitable vessel for the various levels of ordination. With refuge and a stable mind based on renunciation one is able to adopt any of the seven types of precepts for individual liberation.

The third is that the forces of previously accumulated negative karma and obscurations are purified. A popular anecdote illustrating this point is given in the scriptures. There was once a *devaputra*[37] who foresaw that in his next life he would be reborn as a pig. Deeply apprehensive, he turned to the Three Jewels for guidance and inspiration. The result was that this inauspicious rebirth was avoided. The force of his refuge purified the negative karmic seeds and the spiritual obscurations that would have acted as the cause for the lower rebirth. With these forces overcome, he avoided an unpleasant destiny. On this theme one of the sutras says,

Those who take refuge in the buddhas
Are not reborn in the lower realms.

When they leave behind this human body
They reincarnate in a higher world.

This same idea applies equally to refuge in the Dharma and the sangha.

The fourth beneficial effect is that one will gain a vast store of positive karmic energy. To repeat the words of *The Dharani of the Immortal Drumbeat,*

The accomplished buddhas are inconceivable,
The holy Dharma is inconceivable,
The exalted sangha is inconceivable,
Their beneficial effects are inconceivable.

Fifthly, one will not take rebirth in any of the lower realms. The sutra passage quoted earlier on this point is equally relevant here:

Those who take refuge in the buddhas
Are not reborn in the lower realms.
When they leave behind this human body
They reincarnate in a higher world.

Sixthly, malicious humans and non-humans will no longer cause us harm. A sutra says,

Many people, when moved by fear,
Run to mountains, jungles,
Hermitages, shrines and trees
In search of safety and asylum.

But these are no real refuge
And they afford no real protection.
In the end those who rely upon them
Do not achieve freedom from misery.

But if sometime someone turns for refuge
To the buddhas, the Dharma and the sangha,

And with eyes of wisdom sees the nature
Of the four exalted and noble truths—

The truth of suffering, the source of suffering,
The cessation of every level of suffering,
And the joyous truth of the noble eightfold path—
That person achieves nirvana itself.

This is the real refuge,
And it affords supreme protection.
And in the end those who rely upon it
Become freed from every suffering.

The seventh beneficial effect given in the oral tradition is that through refuge one's every aspiration becomes fulfilled. Whenever one engages in any spiritual activity one should first meditate on refuge and pay reverence to the Three Jewels. Then offer a prayer that the undertaking be successful. Your wishes will be fulfilled as desired.

The eighth is that eventually one will achieve the state of full and perfect enlightenment. This is pointed out in a sutra, "With conviction, personal limitations quickly fade...," and so forth. In other words, through conviction in the efficacy of relying upon the Three Jewels one turns for refuge and achieves a human rebirth. This is a life form especially conducive to making progress on the spiritual path, and through utilizing it wisely one can achieve the sublime state of complete and perfect buddhahood.

One should cultivate awareness of these many beneficial effects of the Three Jewels, and recite the refuge formula three times each day and three times each night.

(vi) The sixth advice is that one should never forsake one's refuge, neither in jest nor at the risk of one's life. Eventually one will be parted from this life, this body, and all one's possessions. But if one allows oneself to become parted from one's commitment to spiritual values the negative effects will carry over into many future lifetimes, and great misery will be experienced. Therefore never forsake your refuge, at any cost whatsoever.

The purpose of generating a healthy concern for the sufferings of the lower realms is to bring a more realistic perspective to the innate instinct we all have to avoid suffering and to achieve happiness. From negative actions of body, speech and mind are produced the karmic seeds that eventually ripen upon us as suffering; and from the positive karmic seeds that we collect come happiness and joy. We should meditate upon the ways that make firm this knowledge. *A Guide to the Bodhisattva Ways* states,

> Misery is born from negative actions.
> "But how can I achieve certain freedom from that?"
> At all times during the day and night
> I should think only of this question.

And also elsewhere (in the same text),

> Buddha himself called spiritual conviction
> The root of all positive ways.
> In order to make that root grow firm
> Meditate on the evolutionary nature of suffering.

By what means is this spiritual conviction aroused? It is born in reliance upon the teachings, the enlightenment transmission. The fully accomplished buddhas directly perceive the most subtle workings of the karmic laws of cause and effect. They speak of the sufferings of the lower realms because of their great compassion for all living beings, and a buddha does not distort the truth.

We should first observe how suffering comes from negativity, and happiness from goodness. Then we should abandon negativity and cultivate the good.

3. PURIFYING THE MIND OF NEGATIVE KARMA

Undoubtedly we carry within ourselves a great store of negative karmic seeds from the past. And even now from time to time we fall under the spell of thoughtlessness and consequently commit negative actions. We should purify ourselves of these karmic seeds by means of applying the four opponent forces. As is said in *The Sutra Revealing the Four Dharmas*,[38]

> The buddhas and bodhisattvas mastered the four opponent forces. These four outshone the power of the negative karmic seeds that had been accumulated (prior to their enlightenment).
> And what are these four? They are the force of regret, application of the antidotal practices, the resolve to turn away from negative ways, and the force of reliance.

Thus the four opponent forces are identified as: *(A)* the force of regret, *(B)* application of the antidotal practices, *(C)* the resolve to turn away from negative ways, and *(D)* the force of reliance.

A) The Force of Regret

Purifying the mind by means of engaging the force of regret means that one contemplates the undesirable karmic effects of negative actions, reflecting upon the ripening karmic effects, the results that coincide with the nature of the cause, and the overall workings of the process.[39]

B) The Application of the Antidote

There are six antidotal practices to be applied in order to purify the mind of the seeds of negative karma. These are as follows:

(i) The first is mentioned in *The Ornament of Mahayana Sutras:* "Holding or reading the profound sutras, such as *The Sutra on the Perfection of Wisdom*."[40]

(ii) Next is meditation on emptiness, etc.[41] Meditations such as those on emptiness are direct antidotes to the influence that the seeds of negative karma have upon us. Being mindful of and meditating upon emptiness leads to the transcendence of the patterns of ego-grasping, which is the root of all negative activity.

(iii) The third purification practice is the recitation of mantras and so forth. This refers to the special tantric mantras and dharanis associated with spiritual purification, such as the one-

hundred-syllable mantra of Vajrasattva, etc.[42] These should be applied in accordance with the stages of meditation and ritual generally taught in the tradition. *The Sutra Requested by Subahu*[43] states,

> Fire which attacks a forest in late summer
> Quickly and easily destroys vast tracts.
> Similarly, when the fires of mantra and dharani
> Are stirred by the winds of self-discipline,
> The heat of the blaze eagerly consumes
> The vast forest of negative karmic seeds.

One should continue the mantra or dharani recitation until signs of purification manifest in one's dreams.

(iv) The fourth antidotal practice is to create images of enlightenment. This means that, with appreciation for the enlightened beings, one builds or commissions the building of images of the buddhas or bodhisattvas, or of enlightenment monuments (stupas).

(v) The fifth practice is to make offerings to the buddhas or to images of them in order to purify the mind of the instincts of negativity.

(vi) The sixth is to rely on names. This means to recite or recollect the names of the buddhas and bodhisattvas, etc.

C) The Resolve

The third opponent force is to generate the thought of determination to turn away from negative ways in the future. Without this resolve, the purification practices are mere vocal excercises.

D) The Force of Reliance

The fourth opponent force is that of reliance. Here one relies upon taking refuge in the Three Jewels and meditating upon the bodhimind, the altruistic aspiration to highest enlightenment.

How effective are these four opponent forces in their function of purifying the mind of negative karmic seeds? This is determined by a number of factors: whether the practice is done with great or small strength, whether all the four forces are present or not, the strength or weakness of the thought behind the practice, the duration of their application, and so forth.

The effects of the practice of the four opponent forces manifest in a number of ways. Sometimes a karmic seed with the potency to bring about great suffering is reduced to the potency of producing only a small suffering. Or one may still take rebirth in a lower realm, but will not experience the unpleasantness generally concomitant with such an incarnation. Also, karmic seeds that could have brought about a lower rebirth now ripen in this lifetime as a mere headache. Or the lower birth that would have had to be endured for a long period of time now becomes of short duration.

The need for purification through the four opponent forces is given in a sutra:

> The karmic seeds within living beings
> Do not perish, even in a hundred aeons.

It may seem contradictory to quote this scriptural passage, in which we are told that karmic seeds are never lost, while at the same time speaking of rendering karmic seeds impotent. However, there is no contradiction. In general the potencies of karmic seeds remain until they are worked out; but this refers only to those, as in the above quotation, that were not purified by means of the four opponent forces.

Also we sometimes see it said in the scriptures that "there is no option but eventually to face the ripening effects of our karma...." It is important to note that this refers to those karmic seeds that have already ripened upon us as undesirable effects in this life, such as being blind. The four opponent forces negate the effects of dormant karmic seeds, not of those that have already been activated.

How long should we meditate upon the karmic laws of cause and effect? At the moment we regard worldly activities as our priority; spiritual endeavor is given a secondary place. We should meditate on karma until this becomes reversed: until our priority becomes spiritual development and worldly activities become of secondary concern.

D. CONTEMPLATING THE UNSATISFACTORY NATURE OF CYCLIC EXISTENCE

Is it sufficient to transcend negativity, the cause of lower rebirth, and to cultivate goodness, the cause of higher rebirth? The answer is no, this is not a sufficient achievement. The entirety of samsaric existence is by its very nature suffering, and therefore we should strive to achieve the state of liberation, which has transcended all samsaric sufferings.

As for why it is said that all of samsara is in the nature of suffering, we can see how this is true as regards the lower realms by what was said earlier (in the description of those realms). But it is equally true concerning the higher realms.

Contemplation of the sufferings of the higher samsaric realms is discussed under three headings: (1) the sufferings of the human realm; (2) those of the *asuras* or antigods; and (3) those of the *devas* or celestial beings.

1. CONTEMPLATING THE SUFFERING OF THE HUMAN REALM

All the varieties of misery and pain that exist in the three lower realms of samsara also exist in the world of humans. We have the sufferings of birth, sickness, aging and death; encountering unpleasant and malicious people; being separated from those we love; the pains of hunger and thirst, heat and cold; and so forth. *The Collected Sayings of the Buddha* states,

> All sufferings found in the lower realms
> Seem to exist in this world of humans.

In general, prosperous humans mainly experience mental sufferings, such as anxiety and stress. For those less prosperous, suffering principally manifests as physical hardships. Both suffer every day in one of these two ways. *The Four Hundred Verses*[44] states,

The prosperous experience misery of the mind;
Ordinary people experience it within the body.
The beings of this world are daily struck
By these two terrible sufferings.

2. CONTEMPLATING THE SUFFERING OF THE REALM OF
ASURAS

The unsatisfactory nature of the realm of the asuras is described
in (Nagarjuna's) *Letter to a Friend,*

By nature the asuras are intensely envious
Of the glory of the devas; the consequence is misery.
Though intelligent, due to the limits of their world
They are unable to discern higher levels of truth.

The asuras, or antigods, are miserly even with their own
daughters. Fiercely jealous of the superior glories of the god
realms, they seem constantly to be waging war. As a result they
suffer from wounds on their limbs and bodies. Moreover, this
realm of life provides no opportunity for the cultivation of
spiritual vision.

3. THE SUFFERINGS OF THE DEVA REALMS

The sufferings experienced by the gods are of two types: those
experienced in the heavens of sensuality, and those experienced
in the higher heavens.
Concerning the first of these *A Letter to a Friend* states,

The pleasures of the devas are intense indeed,
But more intense are their sufferings at death.

As said here, even though the devas of the sensual heavens
have great pleasures, the five sufferings that come to them as they
approach their death are even greater. What are the five? They
must watch the beauty of their skin fade, the flower garlands
of their glory wither, and they become unable to sit at ease.
Their once flawless garb becomes stained, and their once stain-
less bodies begin to perspire and become unclean in other ways.

As for the higher gods, or those who have taken birth as a deva of the form or formless realms, they also do not pass beyond the reach of pain. Although they have transcended gross negativity and so do not experience actual sensations of suffering, nonetheless a subtle level of mental distortion and delusion still exists within their mindstreams. Moreover, they do not have the power to remain in the celestial realms forever. Sooner or later they must die; and then they must reincarnate, possibly even into one of the three lower realms. Like an arrow shot into the sky which falls back to earth once its throwing power is expended, when the karmic forces that threw them into the celestial realms have burned themselves out these beings fall back into the lower realms of existence. They then experience all the miseries concomitant with the unenlightened, samsaric world.

Thus regardless of which of the three dimensions of the world one is born into, it is yet another place of misery. No matter who one's companion, one is always accompanied by suffering. And no matter what possessions one may collect or what pleasures one may indulge in, they do not pass beyond the reach of dissatisfaction. As everything in samsara is by nature suffering we should strive to attain the state of spiritual liberation that has transcended all states of distortion and proneness to pain.

To transcend all states of samsaric imperfection and suffering we must begin by recognizing the cause of this suffering. And what is this cause?

It is twofold: contaminated karmic forces and the deluded nature of the mind. The latter is the principal of these two; for when delusion is not present the forces of karma are rendered impotent, and when delusion is present we continue to collect the karmic instincts that will act as the seeds of future samsaric rebirths.

Well then, how does one eliminate the forces of delusion? This is accomplished by means of taking up the practices of the three higher trainings: self-discipline, meditative absorption and wisdom.

Point Two: The Actual Practice, Cultivating the Two Bodhiminds

As said above, through practice of the three higher trainings one may attain to personal spiritual liberation. But is this a sufficient attainment?

The answer is a categorical no. With personal liberation one will have transcended clinging to the glitter of samsaric indulgence; yet because more remains both to be transcended and to be achieved, one has not yet ultimately fulfilled either one's own purposes or one's responsibilities toward the world.

Therefore eventually one will have to enter into the practice of the Mahayana, the Great Way. This being so, those with wisdom enter into this path from the very beginning of their training. Moreover the sole door entering into the Mahayana is cultivation of the bodhimind, the thought of enlightenment, the aspiration to achieve buddhahood for the benefit of all living beings. The wise therefore begin by cultivating this extraordinary attitude.

Why is the bodhimind called the sole door to the Mahayana? Because even if one has not yet gained realization of qualities such as meditative absorption or the wisdom of emptiness, the mere presence of the bodhimind places one upon the Mahayana path.

Conversely, one may have gained qualities such as meditative absorption and the wisdom of emptiness, but if the force of the bodhimind degenerates within one's mindstream one falls from the Great Way.

When a practitioner dwells within the bodhimind, the smallest act of generosity, such as giving a morsel of food to an animal or insect, becomes a bodhisattva practice. Conversely, when one lacks the bodhimind even the most profound practice fails to become a bodhisattva activity. Methods such as meditative absorption, the contemplation of profound emptiness, self-identification as a tantric divinity, the powerful tantric yogas that work with the subtle energies and channels, etc., no longer qualify as Mahayana endeavors.

Consequently those who wish to accomplish the Great Way to enlightenment begin by taking up the practices for cultivating the bodhimind.

The bodhimind itself is of two types: conventional and ultimate. The former of these mainly refers to the state of mind based on love and compassion that aspires to achieve full enlightenment as the supreme means of benefiting all living beings; the latter refers to the wisdom that perceives voidness, the deeper nature of existence, the emptiness nature of the self and phenomena.

Thus the actual training has two aspects: (I) cultivating the conventional bodhimind, the altruistic aspiration to highest enlightenment, and (II) cultivating the ultimate bodhimind, the wisdom of emptiness.

I. CULTIVATING THE CONVENTIONAL BODHIMIND

The discussion of the training in the conventional bodhimind involves four topics: (A) the causes giving rise to the bodhimind; (B) the actual steps in the training; (C) the measure of progress; and (D) the ritual for formally committing oneself to the bodhisattva ideal, which is the rite for generating the bodhisattva resolve.

A. THE CAUSES GIVING RISE TO THE BODHIMIND

In his *Compendium of Bodhisattva Trainings*[45] the (Indian) master Shantideva speaks of *(1)* four conditions, *(2)* four causes and *(3)* four strengths by which the bodhimind is aroused.

1. The four conditions are as follows.

(a) One hears of or sees the amazing splendor of the buddhas and bodhisattvas, and as a consequence experiences the thought, "I too must attain that state of enlightenment for the benefit of the world."

(b) Perhaps one does not have a direct experience such as is described above, yet on reading or hearing the scriptures of the Great Way becomes inspired by the wondrous descriptions of the buddhas and bodhisattvas and thus engenders the altruistic aspiration to enlightenment.

(c) In some people neither of these two conditions occur, yet they become overwhelmed by concern for the spiritual state of the world. Unable to bear the thought of the enlightenment methods disappearing from within the world, they resolve to master the teachings and achieve enlightenment in order to help preserve the spiritual way.

(d) Lastly, in some people the bodhimind arises purely from appreciation of the tremendous beauty and rarity of the bodhisattva spirit. They think to themselves, "The spiritual ways of the shravakas and pratyekabuddhas may be rare, but how much more rare is the exalted bodhimind!" Within this sphere of appreciation they experience an intense wish to achieve the bodhisattva ideal.

2. The four causes are explained as follows: *(a)* strong karmic instincts from previous lifetimes, which infuse one's mindstream with Mahayana tendencies; *(b)* the guidance of a Mahayana master; *(c)* a compassionate mind for other living beings; and *(d)* a spirit that does not become fatigued with the challenges that beset a practitioner who has resolved to accomplish the Great Way.

3. The four strengths: (a) personal strength, i.e., through one's own efforts one cultivates the thought of enlightenment; *(b)* the strength of others, i.e., the inspiration of a spiritual friend causes one to aspire to highest enlightenment; *(c)* causal strength, which refers to instincts from past lifetimes that act as a cause of the enlightenment thought; and *(d)* applied strength, which is the force of meditation and familiarity applied in this lifetime.

B. THE ACTUAL STEPS IN THE TRAINING

There are two principal means for generating the conventional bodhimind: (1) that known as the "Sevenfold Oral Tradition Technique of Cause and Effect," and (2) that known as the "Oral Tradition Method of Exchanging Self-cherishing for the Cherishing of Others."

1. THE SEVENFOLD ORAL TRADITION TECHNIQUE

The seven steps in this method are: recognizing all sentient beings as having once been one's mother; recollecting the kindness of the mother; generating the thought to repay this kindness; generating love, that sees all beings as precious; generating compassion; generating the extraordinary attitude of universal responsibility; and giving rise to the bodhimind itself, the altruistic thought of enlightenment. It is on the basis of this seventh step that the state of highest enlightenment is eventually attained.

The above sevenfold technique will be discussed under two general topics: *(A)* the spiritual character that is to be generated throughout the training; and *(B)* the actual stages in practice.

A) The Spiritual Character That Is To Be Generated

This is discussed under two headings: *(1)* how compassion is the root of the Great Way; and *(2)* how the seven factors function as cause and effect.

(1) How Compassion is the Root of the Great Way

Great compassion is fundamental in the beginning stages of Mahayana training, for one's sense of universal concern depends upon it; and without a sense of universal concern there is no way to enter into the Great Way. The above assertion is supported by reason; for it is through the force of great compassion that one resolves to free all living beings from samsaric misery. When one's compassion is weak, this resolve does not arise.

The Sutra of Unfading Wisdom[46] states, "The great compassion of the bodhisattva is the perfect preliminary to entering into the Great Way." Also we read in *The Sutra of the Sacred Mountain*,[47] "The starting point of all bodhisattva activities is cultivation of great compassion."

Great compassion is equally important throughout the course of the Mahayana training. One may achieve an initial experience of compassion, yet if one does not follow through by repeatedly familiarizing onself with and reinforcing it, there is the danger that one will become overwhelmed by the limitless number of living beings and by their many ostensible imperfections. Also, one can easily become fatigued by the extent of the trainings to be accomplished and difficulties faced during the course of practice. The possible consequence is a fall to a lesser path.

Conversely when one meditates regularly on great compassion one becomes oblivious to concern with personal happiness and becomes unshakably stable in the altruistic bodhisattva deeds. This in turn causes all spiritual qualities to increase within one's mindstream.

Finally, great compassion is indispensable to the completion of the Great Way. Enlightenment without the presence of great compassion refers to the complacent, personal nirvana of the shravaka arhats and pratyekabuddhas. It is the force of great compassion that provides the added impetus to transform this experience into the full illumination of omniscient buddhahood and that inspires the strength to work for all sentient beings until samsara has been emptied.

If we wish to cultivate a particular plant then in the beginning we must acquire a fertile and specific seed. In the middle we must ensure that the sprout receives the correct amount of water, sunlight, fertilizer and so forth. Finally in the end sustained growth is necessary to bring the plant to the stages of flowering and bearing fruit.

Similarly in the beginning of our practice of the Great Way

great compassion is the seed. In the middle, it is the water, sunlight and moisture. Then in the end it is the sustaining force that brings forth all the enlightenment activities.

The (Indian Buddhist master Chandrakirti writes in his) treatise *A Guide to the Middle View*,[48]

> In the vast harvest of buddhas, compassion is the
> seed;
> It is also the water and so forth that grows the
> seed;
> And it is the sustaining power that brings the
> plant to fruition.
> Therefore I first pay homage to great compassion.

(2) How the Seven Factors Function as Cause and Effect

This is discussed under two headings: *(a)* how the first five stages, from recognizing all living beings as one's mother up to cultivating the love that sees them all as precious, function as causes; and *(b)* how universal responsibility and the bodhimind are the results.

(a) How the first five factors function as causes

It is said that compassion is easily generated by meditating repeatedly upon the sufferings to which all sentient beings are prone. But in order for this compassion to be stable in its immediacy and intensity, one must first make firm the mind of universal love that sees all living beings as precious and dear.

Why? Because at the moment when we see that someone whom we regard as harmful to us has encountered difficult circumstances we rejoice in his or her misfortune. Moreover, when we see a stranger encounter difficulties our only emotional response is apathy. It is solely for friends and relatives that we have a genuine concern. We lack the consciousness that sees all living beings as precious.

This sense of empathy, that at the moment is limited to our small circle of loved ones, must be extended until it encompasses all living beings without any partiality. This is the mind that serves as the basis for the experience of great compassion.

The quality that we want to bring into our relationship with all sentient beings is that of a close friend or a deeply beloved relative. It is for this reason that we meditate upon all others as being friends and relatives. This encourages the birth of the attitude of love, that sees all other beings as beautiful.

Moreover, the closest of all friends is the mother, for the kindness of a mother to a child surpasses all other kindnesses. It is for this reason that the first of the seven steps in the sevenfold technique is the meditation of imagining that all sentient beings have once been one's mother.

From the awareness that all beings have been one's mother, together with awareness of the tremendous kindness of the mother, there arises the aspiration to repay their kindness. This in turn gives rise to the beautiful mind of impartial love that acts as the foundation stone of great compassion unable to bear the sufferings of others.

(b) How the last two factors function as effects
The above five factors—recognizing all beings as having once been one's mother, generating awareness of the kindness of the mother, giving birth to the thought to repay their kindness, and generating love and compassion—then act as the basis of the last two factors in the sevenfold process: the extraordinary attitude of universal responsibility; and the bodhimind, the aspiration to highest enlightenment as the supreme means of benefiting others.

Some teachers have stated that there is no need for meditating upon the sixth factor, the extraordinary attitude of universal responsibility. They claim that the bodhimind can arise directly from great compassion.

I do not agree with them. The sixth step in the sevenfold process is an important phase in the process, linking the force of great compassion to one's personal sense of universal commitment. This is an important dynamic in generating the experience of the bodhimind, and it is for this reason that the masters of old recommended it. Hence it should not be glossed over.

How does one meditate on the extraordinary attitude of universal responsibility? After the first five steps of the sevenfold technique have been meditated upon one gives rise to and dwells within the thought, "I will personally contribute to maintaining the happiness of others and to freeing them from suffering. Since beginningless time they have repeatedly been a mother to me, each time bringing me the gift of life and protecting me from harm. Thus all sentient beings have been extremely kind to me. I should personally take upon myself the responsibility of repaying them by showing them only love and compassion, and by fulfilling all of their needs."

The doubt then arises, "How can I possibly fulfill the needs of the world? At the moment I cannot fulfill the needs of even one person, namely myself, so why even mention fulfilling the needs of others? Moreover, even the shravaka arhats and pratyekabuddhas, being but partially accomplished, can fulfill but a fraction of the purposes of the world."

"So who can fulfill all levels of the needs of living beings? Only a buddha, a fully enlightened being, who has transcended all personal limitations and achieved every excellent quality; for one ray of light, one miraculous deed, or one word of instruction from an omniscient being has the power to ripen and awaken countless living beings."

With this realization there arises the thought, "I must myself achieve the state of complete and perfect buddhahood."

It is this determined aspiration that is the seventh step, the conventional bodhimind.

B) The Actual Stages in Practice

There are three principal aspects of the training: *(1)* cultivating the mind which is concerned with the well-being of others; *(2)* cultivating the mind which is concerned with enlightenment; and *(3)* integrating the fruit of the training, the experience of the bodhimind.

(1) Cultivating the Mind Concerned with Others
This involves two trainings: *(a)* preparing the basis which can give birth to this unique aspect of the mind; and *(b)* actually generating it.

(a) Preparing the basis

Preparing the basis involves two levels of practice: developing equaminity toward all living beings; and developing the mind that sees others as precious.

Developing equanimity toward all living beings. To experience the spiritual qualities of universal love that wishes to see all others in happiness, and compassion that wishes to see them all free from suffering, it is necessary first to transcend the habit of responding with attachment or aversion toward the sentient beings; for it is these that create and sustain the syndrome of partiality. Otherwise one's love and compassion will remain discriminatory. The love and compassion that we want to generate here should encompass all sentient beings equally. Therefore the basis that we want to establish is one of complete equanimity, the equanimity that is the third of the four immeasurable spiritual qualities.[49]

From the viewpoint of the beings themselves all are equal, for each considers himself or herself as supremely important. Also from our own viewpoint all are equal, for each has been a mother to us in some past life.

Here we meditate on the latter aspect. In what manner? So as to see all beings without discriminating between friend and foe, near and far. We must learn to see all as equally precious.

As said above, from the viewpoint of the beings themselves they all are equal. All equally want happiness and want to avoid suffering. And from one's own viewpoint all have been a mother to us in one lifetime or another since beginningless time, and on that occasion kindly provided us with life and sustenance.

The focus here should be to eliminate the tendency of seeing beings as either friends or enemies, for there is nobody who has always been a friend to us since beginningless time; nor is there anyone for whom we have always felt enmity.

The meditation proceeds as follows: Begin by visualizing a person toward whom you have no particular emotion whatsoever, toward whom you feel neither friendship nor enmity. Then include friends and relatives, such as your mother and father. Finally, include beings for whom you feel enmity and aversion. The aim is eventually to be able to include all sentient beings within the sphere of your appreciation.

Developing the mind that sees all others as precious. This involves meditation on three of the factors in the sevenfold bodhi-mind technique, namely, *(i)* recognizing that all other sentient beings have once been a mother to us; *(ii)* recollecting the kindness of the mother; and *(iii)* the wish to repay them.

(i) Recognizing all living beings as having been one's mother. Here one contemplates how both oneself and others have experienced an infinite number of previous incarnations since beginningless time. As a consequence one will have had every type of relationship with all other beings. Specifically, each living being will have been a mother to us in one lifetime or another. There is no limit to the beginning of cyclic existence, and therefore our lives, deaths and rebirths are without a limit. A person who has never been a mother to us cannot be found even by an omniscient being.

A scripture states, "Given the extent of past time, there is no place in which any specific sentient being has not been born, has not lived, and has not died. It would be rare to see such a place. Similarly, we have all been father, mother, child, teacher, spiritual guide and friend to one another again and again. It would be hard to find a being with whom we have not shared these relationships."

(ii) Recollecting the kindness of the mother. Here it is customary to take one's mother of this lifetime as the model. Visualize her in the space before you and think, "She has been my mother in all my lives since beginningless time. Again and again she has shown me the kindness of a mother. Especially, in this incarnation she conceived me in her womb. At that time she carefully protected me in every way she could, undergoing great hardship for me, such as observing special dietary and behavioral disciplines solely for my well-being. My birth caused her tremendous pain; yet when I emerged looking more like a slippery red worm than a human being she nonetheless lovingly picked me up in her tender hands and held me to her body to give me warmth. Thereafter she fed and cleaned me, and carefully watched over me throughout my infancy. She gave me food when I was hungry, drink when I was thirsty,

and clothing when I needed protection from the elements. In this way she cared for me at the cost of immense personal sacrifice to herself.

"She even gave me the precious gift of a human life form, thus providing me with a basis capable of receiving the spiritual teachings and engaging in the threefold application of study, contemplation and meditation, the means by which liberation and omniscient enlightenment may be obtained. She would rather face illness herself than see me become ill, and would rather die herself than allow me to die. In brief, she exerted every means at her disposal to benefit me."

One should meditate in this way until an intense sense of appreciation arises. When this occurs, replace the visualization of your mother of this life with that of your father. Meditate how he too has been a mother to you in many past lives, and on those occasions has shown you all the kindnesses of a mother.

Then replace his image with that of friends, relatives, enemies and all other living beings. Meditate how they have all provided you with the many kindnesses of a mother in many previous lifetimes.

(iii) Generating the thought to repay this kindness. Here one begins by recollecting how, even though the mind's memory is blurred by the intense experience of death, intermediate state and rebirth, nonetheless all others have been one's mother and have shown you great kindness.

One then asks oneself the question, "If this is the case, how can I ever be unkind or cruel toward them?" As is said in *A Letter to a Disciple*,[50]

> The living beings tossing in the ocean of samsara
> Are as though caught in a powerful whirlpool.
> They pass from life to death to rebirth,
> Not remembering that in infinite past lifetimes
> They have all been a mother to one another.
> Would it not be ignoble to be uncaring toward them?

To ignore and abandon one's mother is not considered acceptable behavior even to the most coarse and vulgar people.

How then can I not respond to the kindness that all beings have shown to me? I should repay their kindness with kindness.

How can their kindness be repaid? Since beginningless time the beings have experienced all sorts of samsaric delights, yet these were ephemeral and faded away to nothing. What they need is the liberation of eternal happiness. As is said in *Verses Tuned to the Naga King's Drum,*[51]

> The ocean, king of mountains and the mighty
>   continents
> Are not heavy burdens to bear when compared
> To the burden of not repaying the world's
>   kindness.
> Those who are not ignoble understand this
> And work for the good of the world.
> The kindness of living beings is not wasted on
>   them,
> And they are praised by the wise as supreme.

That is to say, the thought to repay others by acting toward them in accordance with the ways of enlightenment is praised by the wise as the supreme response.

b. Actually generating the mind concerned with others

This process is accomplished by the next three steps in the sevenfold technique: *(iv)* meditation upon love, that sees others as precious; *(v)* meditation upon compassion, that wishes to see them free from suffering; and *(vi)* meditation upon the thought of universal responsibility.

(iv) Meditation upon love. Here one simply dwells in the thought, "May those beings bereft of happiness come to possess happiness, and may they remain in happiness."

The benefits of meditation upon the thought of love are described in *The King of Absorptions Sutra,*

> One may make offerings every day
> Equal in size to a million world systems,
> To all the holy, enlightened beings;

Yet this will not generate the meritorious energy
Created by one session of meditation upon love.

Also elsewhere it is said, "One may dwell in the bliss of
meditative absorption equal to that found in the buddhafields,
or live as a monk or a nun for a billion aeons; but neither of
these activities will generate the meritorious energy created by
a single session of meditation in samadhi on the theme of love."

Moreover in *A Precious Garland*[52] the (Indian) master Nagarjuna states that a practitioner who meditates on the thought
of universal love is a delight to both humans and divine beings; consequently he or she gains the excellent fortune of divine protection.

The meditation on love should first be practiced by taking
one's mother as the visualized model. Then successively visualize
father, relatives, friends, acquaintances, strangers, enemies, and
all sentient beings. One contemplates that each of them has been
one's mother in some past life; yet seeing that they are now
bereft of happiness one makes the aspiration, "May they have
happiness and its causes. May they always dwell in happiness."

The sign of progress in this meditation is that one begins
to wish happiness for all other beings as intensely as a parent
wishes happiness for an only child.

(v) Meditation upon compassion. One dwells within the aspiration, "May all the living beings afflicted by suffering become free from suffering and its causes. May they always dwell
in freedom from suffering."

The beneficial effects of meditation upon compassion are
equal to those arising from meditation upon love, as described
above.

The meditation proceeds in a similar manner to that on love,
beginning by visualizing one's mother and eventually including all beings. Meditate upon the ways in which they experience
suffering in their lives. Then make the aspiration that they
be freed from all suffering and sorrow.

The sign of progress in the meditation is that one begins
to feel compassion for others as intensely as a mother would
feel it for an only child afflicted by pain.

(vi) The extraordinary attitude of universal responsibility. Here one contemplates the thought, "May beings in states of suffering be freed from them; may all beings come to dwell in happiness. May I myself contribute to these two goals in every possible way."

Thus the first six steps of the sevenfold technique are classified as methods for generating the mind that takes an interest in the well-being of others, that is, in the welfare of the world. And it is on this basis that one generates the mind that takes an interest in enlightenment.

(2) Cultivating the Mind Concerned with Enlightenment

When meditation upon the above six steps has achieved a degree of maturity the thought spontaneously arises, "I wish to accomplish what is beneficial to all living beings; but in fact only a buddha, a fully enlightened being, is really able to do so in every way and on all levels. Therefore for the benefit of all living beings I will strive to attain the peerless state of supreme enlightenment."

This is a simple way of performing the sevenfold meditation for generating the conventional bodhimind. It is an effective means of giving birth to the enlightenment aspiration, the bodhisattva perspective.

(3) Integrating the Fruit of the Training

The final fruit of the sevenfold technique is the generation of the aspirational bodhimind, the altruistic dedication to highest enlightenment. The nature of this aspiration is neither exclusively to benefit the world nor exclusively to attain enlightenment oneself; rather, it is a combination of the two ideals: one strives for enlightenment as a means of benefiting the world.

This is the nature of the aspirational bodhimind. Once it has been generated one can take up the applicational bodhimind, or the bodhimind that engages in the bodhisattva practices such as the six perfections: generosity, discipline, patience, enthusiastic effort, meditative stabilization and wisdom. It is the presence of the aspirational bodhimind that transforms these activities into bodhisattva practices and into causes of enlightenment.

The nature of the applicational bodhimind is succinctly described in *The Ornament of Clear Realizations:*[53]

The aspirational bodhimind is the wish
To achieve full and complete enlightenment
As a means to benefit the world.

As for the twofold division of the bodhimind into aspirational and applicational aspects, these are described as follows in *A Guide to the Bodhisattva Ways,*

When the conventional bodhimind is subdivided
It has two aspects: aspirational and applicational.
One of these is like the wish to travel to a distant city;
The other like the motions that transport one there.

Thus the conventional bodhimind has two aspects: one related to aspiration and the other to practical application. As for these two, it is the altruistic aspiration to highest enlightenment that acts as the basis for both.

A technical note may be relevant here. It is said that regardless of whether or not one engages in the bodhisattva practices, such as the six perfections, one's level remains that of the aspirational bodhimind until one's mindstream becomes reinforced by the vow to accomplish the bodhisattva ways. Only when the aspirational bodhimind is coupled with the formal commitment to abide within the bodhisattva practices is it fully characterized as the applicational bodhimind.

The first section of (Kamalashila's) *The Stages of Meditation*[54] puts it this way:

The wish to achieve buddhahood for the benefit of the infinite number of sentient beings is the aspirational bodhimind. If on top of that one takes the vow to accomplish the bodhisattva ways and consequently strives to abide within the collections of merit and wisdom, one has entered into the domain of the applicational bodhimind.

This concludes my treatment of how to generate the bodhi-mind by means of the method known as "The Sevenfold Oral Tradition Technique of Cause and Effect." I will now move on to the oral tradition method known as "The Technique of Exchanging Self-Awareness for Awareness of Others."

2. EXCHANGING SELF-AWARENESS FOR AWARENESS OF OTHERS

The technique for generating the bodhimind through exchanging self-awareness for awareness of others is presented under three headings: *(A)* the benefits of cultivating a universal attitude and the disadvantages of not doing so; *(B)* the ability of the mind to transform egotism through familiarity with meditation upon exchanging self-awareness for awareness of others; and *(C)* the stages in the meditation upon this exchange.

A) The Benefits of Doing So and the Faults of Not

Self-cherishing is said to be the source of all conflicts in this world. The cherishing of others is said to be the source of all happiness. *A Guide to the Bodhisattva Ways* puts it this way:

> All the happiness that exists
> Arises from wishing joy for others;
> And all the misery that exists
> Arises from wishing happiness for oneself alone.

> What more need be said?
> The spiritually immature think of themselves alone,
> Whereas the buddhas think only of others.
> Look at the difference between the two.

And also elsewhere in the same text:

> If one is unable to transform obsession for pleasure
> Into genuine concern for the plight of others,
> There is no hope to achieve enlightenment;
> And even in worldly affairs there is no joy.

B) The Mind's Ability to Transform Egotism

Overcoming self-cherishing in itself strengthens the tendency of cherishing others, for the two are natural opposites: self-cherishing is the source of all negativity, and the cherishing of others is the source of all creative relationships. When the former has been eliminated, the latter has few obstacles to its growth.

It may be argued that although in theory this may be true, in actual fact the thought of cherishing others arises but rarely and therefore there is no opportunity to really familiarize the mind with it.

This line of criticism may have some basis in truth as far as a person not engaged in a disciplined practice is concerned, for indeed it is not easy to generate the mind that cherishes all living beings. But it can be achieved through meditational endeavor; for through sustained meditation upon cherishing others one becomes increasingly familiar with the subject of the meditation. For example, it is not easy to change a relationship of suspicion and enmity into one of trust and friendship, but it can be accomplished if one dedicates oneself to the task and becomes increasingly familiar with the other person within the framework of a warm and creative environment. In fact one can become so close to that other person, whose presence previously had caused only apprehension and discomfort, that in the end one misses him or her should he or she move away to some other part of the country. Self-cherishing inspires us to strive for our own happiness and well-being; the cherishing of others inspires us to strive for the happiness and well-being of others. Usually we place all the emphasis on the former instinct. But both forces are equally valid, for both oneself and others are equal in wanting to abide in happiness and well-being, and are equal in wanting to remain free from suffering.

Therefore practitioners of the Great Way learn to see that all beings are equal in their wish to attain happiness and to avoid suffering; and they no longer consider their own interests as being above those of everyone else.

You may think, "There is no need for me to be concerned

with the well-being of others, for any suffering that they may experience does not decrease my happiness, nor does their happiness benefit me in any way. In fact the situation is quite to the contrary; self-cherishing is very useful to me, for my own happiness and pleasure benefits me directly, and any suffering or pain that I experience harms me directly."

However, to accept this line of reasoning as valid contradicts the logic of undertaking any constructive, responsible action whatsoever. As we are in a constant state of change, the self of the future cannot be said to be the same entity as the self of the present; so why should the self of the present (which is one entity) initiate any action now that will only benefit the self of the future (which is a different entity)? By the time any action produces its result, the original creator of the action has already transformed and thus will no longer exist (as the same entity). The person who experiences the fruition of the action is no longer the same person as the one who initiated the action.

Not to acknowledge the import of universal responsibility is like saying there is no need for the hand to make any effort to remove a pain afflicting the foot on the grounds that the pain does not affect the hand!

Perhaps we will argue that neither of these illustrations are valid; for the selves of the present and future have one stream of being, and the hand and foot are part of the same entity, whereas myself and others are two entirely different, unconnected categories of phenomena. However, this argument is also ineffective; for the stream connecting conscious moments and the separate parts of an aggregate have themselves no real existence and therefore are just as unrelated.

What exactly does it mean to exchange self-awareness for awareness of others? Not that one thinks one is someone else, nor that someone else's eye, for example, is one's own eye.

The concept is that ordinary, untrained and spiritually undeveloped people generally are concerned only for themselves and their immediate loved ones, with no sense of responsibility whatsoever for the well-being of the other sentient beings. It is this tendency that is to be transformed and reversed. We want to become more concerned with the happiness of others, to learn to cherish all other living beings and wish them well, even at the cost of the occasional personal sacrifice.

C) The Stages in Meditation upon the Exchange

The meditation proceeds in four steps: *(1)* identifying the object of all blame; *(2)* meditating on the kindness of others; *(3)* cherishing others; and *(4)* the actual exchange of self awareness for awareness of others.

(1) Identifying the Object of All Blame
The object to be blamed for the frustrations, difficulties and sufferings that we experience is identified as follows in the root text:

Place all blame upon one object.

All harms and difficulties that befall us essentially have their source in the self-cherishing attitude. It is the self-cherishing attitude that is at the root of the sufferings we experience because of harms caused by humans and non-humans. Even the sufferings we experience as a result of illness, and all the terrors and fear that we experience, have self-cherishing as their supporting condition.

We do not need to put the blame anywhere outside ourself, for it is right here within our own stream of consciousness. Since beginningless time we have held attachment to personal comfort and pleasure as our supreme goal. As a result we have created endless negative karma with this end in mind, being constantly drawn into an endless vicious struggle in order to get what we "want" and avoid what we "don't want." But the actual result has been the opposite; this grasping, instead of fulfilling our desires, has only brought us unwanted suffering, frustration and pain. As is said in a scripture,

All the pain that exists in the world,
All the terror and misery to be found,
Originates from the self-cherishing attitude.
What other ghost needs to be exorcised?

Self-cherishing has not only harmed us in our countless past lives since beginningless time. Even now it continues to harm us. Motivated by it we constantly run after personal comfort and pleasure, and in this effort fall into patterns of deception, cunning and countless vicious games. This leads us into conflicts and the numerous negative karmic actions that ensue.

As we still have not succeeded in eliminating the self-cherishing attitude, we continue to be drawn into the vicious circle of negativity and to throw ourselves into the future amidst a vast whirlpool of unpleasant conditions, sorrow and pain. Therefore we should regard this self-cherishing attitude as our deepest enemy and should make every effort to transcend it.

From the beginning of beginningless time we have been loyal to the self-cherishing attitude, yet it has repaid us only with frustration and misery, and has held us back from the ways of enlightenment. On the other hand, had we directed ourselves instead to the ideal of cherishing others and to eliminating the self-cherishing tendency, we would have achieved the sublime state of buddhahood long ago. The dedication that in the past has been shown to the self-cherishing attitude should, from this moment onward, be shown toward the attitude of cherishing others.

(2) and (3) Meditating on Others' Kindness and Learning to Cherish Them
One begins by visualizing the mother of this life and recollecting how she has been our mother in many previous lives, each time protecting us with kindness. One contemplates the thought, "I should return her kindness with kindness."

But how can one help others? This is accomplished by encouraging them in the ways of joy and positive behavior. The former directly benefits them, and the latter indirectly does so by encouraging them to cultivate the positive karmic seeds that ripen for them in the future as auspicious conditions.

And what harms them? Suffering directly harms them, and negative behavior indirectly does so, for it is the karmic seeds of negative behavior that ripen in the future as suffering and as inauspicious conditions.

Having contemplated like this concerning one's mother, one then changes the subject to include father, relatives, friends, acquaintances, strangers, those toward whom one feels enmity, and eventually all sentient beings. Meditate on how all have been a mother to you and have shown you great kindness.

(4) The Actual Exchange
Once a sense of cherishing others has been generated in the meditation, engage the technique known as "interwoven sending and receiving."

One begins with the meditation of "receiving." The focus here is the world and its inhabitants. One seeks to take their sufferings and difficulties upon oneself, and to give them every happiness and goodness.

Begin by taking on the faults of the external, inanimate world. As you breathe in, visualize that all harsh qualities of the inanimate world, such as thorns, excessive heat and cold, floods, drought, etc., are inhaled in the form of a thick black cloud and come to your heart. This strikes against the self-cherishing tendency, which is visualized as a black ball at the center of the heart.

Then turn your attention to the living beings. As you breathe in, visualize that the specific sufferings of the living beings, as well as their negative karmic seeds, are taken away from them. These negativities come in the form of a black cloud to the center of your heart and eliminate your self-cherishing.

Meditate that in this way the hell beings are released from the sufferings of heat, cold and torture; animals are freed from the sufferings of eating one another, etc.; ghosts are liberated from the sufferings of hunger, thirst, etc.; humans are released from the sufferings of birth, sickness, old age and death; the demigods are freed from the misery of constant conflict, etc.; the sensual gods from the torment of the signs of death, etc.; and the higher gods from the all-pervasive suffering of being based on samsaric aggregates.

Meditate that you also take upon yourself the obscurations still obstructing the complete enlightenment of the shravaka arhats, pratyekabuddhas, and even tenth level bodhisattvas.

However, there is no need to meditate on removing negativities from the buddhas or from one's own spiritual teachers, for the former have already transcended all faults and the latter are to be meditated upon as being perfect in every way. Any faults that appear in one's spiritual teachers, such as sickness, physical disabilities, signs of age, and so forth, should be regarded as mere appearances arising from one's own impure perception. They should be regarded as embodiments of the meditational divinities, the tantric buddhas, and should be considered as having transcended all faults.

Concerning the objects that are taken or received in this meditation, sometimes one can visualize taking upon oneself the specific sufferings of one of the realms of samsara, such as the heat or the torture of the hot hells, etc. Or one can be even more specific, such as meditating upon taking away the misery of one of the hot hells, such as 'Die and Revive.'

Alternatively, sometimes one can visualize separating the beings in one of the six realms from their negative karmic tendencies. Or one can visualize removing their delusions, such as attachment, aversion, etc. Here one can dedicate a complete session to releasing beings from a specific delusion, such as attachment; then in the next session meditate on releasing them from hatred, and so on for the other delusions, such as pride, hesitation, jealousy, miserliness, etc. As before, one meditates that these come in the form of a black cloud and counteract the self-cherishing at the heart.

Next one takes up the mediation of "sending." Again, the subject is the world and its inhabitants. The gifts that one visualizes sending to them include happiness, material objects, one's body of this life, all goodness of the three times, and so forth. One may also visualize sending them the transcendental joy of the buddhas and bodhisattvas, for this by nature is dedicated to the spiritual elevation of the world.

Generally it is considered appropriate to visualize offering only one's body of this life, for one's bodies of past lives are gone and those of future lives have not yet been gained.

It may be argued that the same holds true of meritorious karma, and therefore it is inappropriate to meditate upon giving away all goodness of the three times, for past goodness is gone and future goodness not yet achieved. However, goodness refers to the positive karmic seeds carried on the mindstream, and it is quite valid to meditate on dedicating these to the well-being of others.

The method of performing the meditation of "sending" is as follows: Again one begins with the external, inanimate world. Visualize that it is transformed into a pure land, its surface as exquisite as lapis lazuli studded with gold inlay.

Next consider the living beings that inhabit this world. One begins with the mother of this life, and then gradually extends the scope of the meditation until it includes father, relatives, friends, strangers, enemies, etc., until all living beings are encompassed. Meditate that you give them all happiness and every goodness of the three times.

Sometimes take the hell beings as the object of concentration, sometimes the shravaka arhats, pratyekabuddhas and even tenth level bodhisattvas. Meditate that all of these beings transcend their limitations and move toward enlightenment.

This practice of "sending" is in harmony with the aspirations of the buddhas and spiritual masters, for the holy beings want only happiness for others and wish all beings to be free from suffering.

Here the root text states,

Meditate on interwoven sending and receiving.

This is how the lines read in one version of the text. In another version we find,

In the actual practice, meditate on interwoven sending and receiving;
And begin the receiving with yourself.

The essential meaning of the two readings is the same. The difference is that the second places a greater emphasis upon the "sending and receiving" phase in the overall structure of the training.

The words "begin the receiving with yourself" refer to the practice of accepting all suffering, afflictions and delusions that arise within oneself as forces that purify and bring one release from the karmic seeds that otherwise would cause harm in future lives.

When you have purified your own mindstream in this way, visualize before you your mother of this life. Consider how she has been your mother in countless past incarnations, on each of those occasions bringing you great kindness.

In this life too she carried you in her womb, raised you through childhood and did all in her power to fulfill your needs. She even provided you with the body and spiritual circumstances by which you are able to meet with and practice the path to enlightenment. Moreover she could well become your mother again in some future life. To repay her kindness you should respond by acting only in a manner that is of benefit to her and that protects her from harm.

What is of harm to living beings? Suffering and negative behavior—the former directly, and the latter indirectly. And what is of benefit? Happiness benefits them directly, and positive behavior indirectly does so.

Therefore it is from suffering and negative ways that the living beings need protection, and it is in happiness and positive ways that they need encouragement. These are the means by which one should repay the kindness of others.

Build up the force of this contemplation within your meditation. Then visualize that, as you inhale, all negativities are cut from your mother and come toward you in the form of a black cloud. This black cloud of her sufferings, delusions and negative karma flows in a stream to your heart. Consider that in this way she is freed from all suffering. The black cloud strikes against your own self-cherishing, thus eliminating it from within you.

Then as you exhale visualize that all your happiness and meritorious karmic force are sent forth with your breath. These take the form of a white cloud. The cloud dissolves into your mother, fills her with joy, and causes her to evolve toward enlightenment.

Thus in synchronicity with inhalation one takes on all her sufferings and negativities in the form of a black cloud. Similarly in synchronicity with exhalation one sends her all happiness and meritorious karmic energy in the form of a white cloud. The way to conduct an actual meditation session at this point in the training is to begin by dedicating five or six cycles of the breath to taking on your own future suffering and negativity. Then dedicate five or six cycles to taking on the suffering and negativity of your mother. Each time as you inhale meditate on receiving negativity in the form of a black cloud; and as you exhale visualize sending forth all positive qualities in the form of a white cloud.

Next switch the visualization to your father, dedicating five or six rounds of breathing and visualization with him as the object; and so on for friends, relatives, acquaintances, strangers, those toward whom you feel enmity, and all sentient beings. First consider how all have been kind to you; then move into following the breath with the meditation of "sending and receiving."

The root text states,

Ride upon the moving breath.

In the meditation of "sending and receiving" one places awareness on the breath and inhales, together with the visualization of drawing in a black cloud of suffering and negativity that comes to one's heart and attacks one's self-cherishing attitude. One contemplates that the visualized models, beginning with one's mother and then proceeding to one's father, friends, enemies, etc., are thus freed from negativity and sorrow.

The breath is held at the heart for a few moments and then slowly expelled, together with the visualization of sending out all happiness and meritorious energy to others. This goes forth in the form of a white cloud that dissolves into the visualized model (i.e., mother, friend, strangers, etc.) and causes him/her to gain happiness and move toward enlightenment.

As said above, when the breath has been fully drawn in it should be held for a few moments before being expelled. There are also methods whereby it can be held for longer periods of time. This is usually done in conjunction with the trainings for developing meditative absorption and greatly benefits one's powers of concentration.

A similar linking of visualization with the breathing process is followed for the various models used as the object of meditation (i.e., mother, father, stranger, enemy, etc.).

In particular, if you take as the object of your meditation someone who has harmed you and toward whom you consequently feel enmity, begin by visualizing the person in the space before you and contemplating how he/she has been a parent to you in many past lives and has shown you great kindness. Breathe in a vast cloud of his/her negativities, evil thoughts and unpleasant actions, thus freeing him/her from them. Then breathe out a white cloud of happiness and goodness.

One should conclude the session by resting awareness within the sphere of ungrasping clarity. Alternatively, if you are trained in the meditations on immutable voidness, rest in the sphere of emptiness free from true existence.

As you exhale, visualize giving away your body, possessions, meritorious energy and so forth, imagining that the bodily parts being given become wish-fulfilling gems that bestow everything needed.

Through meditating upon the moving breath in this way, the powers of the distorted, conceptual mind are weakened and the powers of meditative concentration are strengthened. This is an important side-effect of the practice.

The meditation also has connections with the training in awareness of impermanence and death. First we breathe in and take upon ourselves the sufferings, then we breathe out and give happiness. Breathing in is like the first breath of our life, the moment of our emergence into this world; and breathing out is like the last moment of our life, our death, when we exhale our last lungful of air. Thus the method spontaneously heightens our awareness of the impermanence of composite phenomena, especially our body.

It may be argued that this meditation technique of "sending and receiving" is too far removed from reality to be of any value or potency, for there is no way that a meditator sitting on his cushion actually benefits anyone by simply imagining taking misery from others and giving them happiness, that in fact nothing is given or taken except in the mind of the meditator. Here the root text states,

Transcend preconceptions in this practice,
For there are many examples of its effectiveness
Demonstrated in the lives of earlier buddhas.
The scriptural source for this oral tradition method
Is the *Jataka* story of Buddha's previous life
As the traveler Dzewoi Bumo.

That is to say, even though there is no physical exchange with others the meditation does not become valueless. Quite to the contrary, it has the value of generating waves of enlightenment within the mindstream of the practitioner, thus eventually bringing tremendous joy and goodness into the world.

Our own historical Buddha Shakyamuni, as well as all the other buddhas of the past, first developed a mind that cherishes others more than the self, and on the basis of this exchange went on to achieve perfect enlightenment.

For example, the popular legend of Buddha Shakyamuni's earlier incarnation as the navigator Dzewoi Bumo is a great inspiration.[55] This Jataka tale in particular is an early scriptural source for the "sending and receiving" meditation technique based on breath awareness.

During meditational sessions one should recollect the kindness of all mother sentient beings and then engage in the breath-based technique of "sending and receiving" in order to exchange self-cherishing for the cherishing of others.

As for how to practice between meditation sessions, here the root text states,

Practice on the three objects,
Three poisons, and three roots of virtue.
This in brief is the oral precept
For the periods between meditation sessions.
In order to remember this,
Recite it verbally in all daily activities.

That is to say, during formal meditation sessions we should meditate on exchanging self-awareness for the awareness of others. Then between sessions, watch the mind closely and proceed accordingly. For example, when attractive people or things appear to you and as a consequence lust or greed arises, consider how in this world there are many beings similarly disturbed by these afflicted emotions. Generate the thought, "May their desire ripen upon me." Breathe in a black cloud embodying the greed and lust of all sentient beings. This comes to your heart and attacks your self-cherishing attitude, thus freeing the sentient beings from the delusions of greed and lust. Then breathe out a white cloud of non-attachment and joy, which uplifts and inspires them.

From the trainings in guru yoga up to the present point in practice, proceed as described earlier during the actual meditation sessions. And during the periods between sittings dwell within the aspiration, "May the afflictions of others ripen upon me, and may my happiness ripen upon them. May their difficulties come to me, and may my joys be shared by them." Also, constantly offer the prayer, "This rare human incarnation has been found; may it be used meaningfully.... May any happiness that I experience be used as a force to purify the world."[56] And so forth.

One contemplates in the same manner when aversion and anger arise, taking upon oneself these delusions from all other sentient beings and sharing all joy and happiness with them; and also when the delusions of ignorance and close-mindedness arise.

This training is very powerful and has profound effects upon the practitioner, for when the mind is cultivated in this way, the expressions of body and speech automatically become transformed and adopt more sensitive and wholesome modes.

As is said in a scripture, "Wherever the mind goes, the body and speech spontaneously follow." By refining and elevating the mind, our expressions of body and speech are immediately and effortlessly refined.

In fact all six causal steps of the sevenfold technique described earlier for generating the aspirational bodhimind are included in the breath-based method of "sending and receiving."

As outlined earlier, the breathing method begins with the contemplation of how all living beings have once been a mother to us, and how as a mother they showed us the kindness of giving us life and protection; these are also the first two steps in the sevenfold technique. This gives rise to the aspiration to repay them, which is identical to the third step.

Then we ask ourselves how we can repay them, and the answer emerges that it is through giving them joy and goodness. This inspires the aspiration, "May they have happiness and its cause, which is positive behavior." This thought is in the nature of universal love, fourth of the seven factors.

Next there arises the thought of how one can protect them, and the answer emerges that one protects them by helping them become free from suffering and its cause, which is negative behavior. This in turn inspires the aspiration, "May they become freed from suffering and its cause, which is negative behavior of body, speech and mind." This aspiration shares the nature of universal compassion, the fifth factor.

Then the thought arises, "I myself will contribute to giving happiness to others and to eliminating suffering from within the world." This is the sixth causal factor in the sevenfold technique, the extraordinary attitude characterized by a sense of universal responsibility.

The root text then states,

The wish to achieve buddhahood:
Make friends with and cultivate to fruition
This sublime thought, the aspirational bodhimind.

What this refers to is that at this point in the meditation upon exchanging self-cherishing for the cherishing of others, one strongly experiences the aspiration to give happiness to others and to eliminate their suffering. This causes the thought to arise, "But do I actually have the ability to accomplish these two ends?" The answer is obvious. At the moment I do not have the ability to fully benefit even one being. In fact, I am not even able to fulfill all of my own purposes in life, nor to eliminate all levels of negativity from within myself, let alone think of helping others to do so within themselves. Even the mighty shravaka arhats and pratyekabuddhas can fulfill but a fraction of the purposes of life, having achieved only a partial accomplishment.

So who can fully benefit others? Only a buddha, a completely enlightened being; for a single light ray, miraculous deed or word of teaching emanated by a fully enlightened buddha has the power to uplift and liberate countless living beings. Therefore until I achieve enlightenment I will not be fully effective in the world and will not be fully beneficial to others.

This awareness inspires the intense resolve, "For the benefit of all living beings I must achieve the state of full and complete enlightenment." This thought is in the nature of the aspirational bodhimind.

If on top of this one is prepared to take the commitment of the applicational bodhimind, which is the resolve to accomplish the vast and profound bodhisattva practices, such as the six perfections, then one should do so. Then on the basis of this commitment one should abide within the bodhisattva ways.

C. THE MEASURE OF PROGRESS

The measure of success in this meditational technique is that the self-cherishing attitude begins to wane; and love for others spontaneously arises within one's mindstream, crystalizing as the altruistic aspiration to highest enlightenment and the resolution to accomplish the bodhisattva activities, the Great Way.

D. THE RITUAL FOR GENERATING THE BODHISATTVA RESOLVE

This involves three topics: (1) the methods of generating the bodhisattva resolve, which is to be utilized by those who have not previously generated it; (2) the methods of guarding against weakening it, for those who have previously generated it; and (3) the methods of restoring it, should it become weakened.

1. THE METHODS OF GENERATING THE BODHISATTVA RESOLVE

This is explained under three headings: *(A)* the object before whom the resolve is generated, *(B)* the basis who generates it, and *(C)* the actual ritual for doing so.

A) The Object Before Whom the Resolve is Generated

As is said in the scriptures, "Having come into the presence of a spiritual master who possesses the vow of a bodhisattva. . . ." That is to say, one takes up the resolve in the presence of a spiritual friend who himself or herself possesses the bodhisattva vow.

B) The Basis of the Resolve

Although there are certain types of other-dimensional beings who by means of thought and physical means are able to take the vow of the aspirational bodhimind, and thus are a potential basis, here the basis is a person who has generated at least a slight experience of the bodhimind by means of having trained the mind on the stages of the path.

C) The Actual Ritual

This has three phases: *(1)* the ritual preliminaries, *(2)* the actual body of the rite, and *(3)* the concluding procedures.

(1) The Ritual Preliminaries

There are three preliminaries: *(a)* taking the special refuge, *(b)* generating meritorious energy, and *(c)* purifying one's motivation.

(a) Taking special refuge

Taking special refuge involves two procedures: *(i)* preparing the room and arranging an altar, and then *(ii)* making requests, taking refuge and the recitation of the advice of refuge.

(i) In the first of these one begins by cleaning the place well. Then annoint it with the essence of the five elements, and with perfumed water. Arrange flowers on the altar, as well as an image of one of the buddhas, a scripture such as *The Summary*, images of any of the bodhisattvas, and so forth. These can be placed on individual platforms of various heights.

Also, arrange a seat for the master who will lead the ritual. Offer flowers, incense and so forth, and also send forth the symbolic offering of the universe (i.e., the mandala offering).

(ii) As for the second point, one begins by visualizing the guru as being a buddha, kneels in his/her presence, places the

palms of the hands together, and makes the following request:

> O spiritual master: Just as all previous thus-gone, liberated, fully enlightened buddhas, and also the great bodhisattvas abiding on the ten stages, first generated the resolve of achieving peerless, pure perfect enlightenment, so likewise now do I, who am called *Such-and-such*, request you to bestow upon me this same resolve of peerless, pure, perfect enlightenment.

Repeat this request three times.

One then takes refuge. Make firm the thought that, from now until enlightenment is achieved, in order to be of benefit to all living beings, you will look to the buddhas as the revealers of refuge, to the Dharma as the actual refuge, and to the sangha as friends helping to accomplish refuge.

On this basis repeat the following words:

> O spiritual master, grant me your attention. I, who am called *Such-and-such*, from now until the essence of enlightenment is achieved, turn for refuge to the supreme of beings to walk this earth, the fully enlightened buddhas; I turn for refuge to the supreme of spiritual paths, the Dharma which brings inner peace and freedom from all clinging; I turn for refuge to the supreme community, the sangha, who have irreversibly achieved the high bodhisattva stages.

These words of refuge are recited three times. Here the passage "O spiritual master. . ." etc., until "the essence of enlightenment is achieved," should also be repeated before each of two subsequent recitations of the refuge formula (rather than, as is sometimes done, just reciting it the first time, and on the subsequent two recitations abbreviating the formula by omitting it and simply chanting "I turn for refuge. . .etc.).

The master then reads out the advice of refuge, as was explained earlier (in the section on taking refuge).

(b) Generating meritorious energy
For this one offers the seven-limbed prayer from *The Aspiration of Samantabhadra* (as appeared in the guru yoga preliminary meditation), to the present and past lineage gurus, the buddhas, and the bodhisattvas.

(c) Purifying one's motivation
One generates the thought of love, the aspiration that all beings have happiness; and then the thought of compassion, the aspiration that all beings be free of suffering.

(2) The Actual Body of the Ritual
One recites the following liturgy three times:

> O buddhas and bodhisattvas residing throughout all ten directions, grant me your attention. O spiritual master, grant me your attention.
> I, who am called *Such-and-such*, take whatever root of meritorious energy I have generated in this life, lives past, and lives to come, through practices such as generosity, self-discipline, meditation, and so forth, or through encouraging others to practice, or through rejoicing in witnessing other beings practice. Just as all past thus gone, liberated, fully accomplished buddhas, and all past bodhisattvas residing on the ten stages, have taken this root of merit and turned it toward giving birth to the thought of peerless, perfect, complete enlightenment, so now do I, who am called *Such-and-such*, from now until the essence of enlightenment is achieved, resolve to cultivate the mind of peerless, perfect and complete enlightenment. I will bring liberation to beings not liberated, will bring freedom to beings not free, will bring breath to those unable to breathe, and will take beyond sorrow those not beyond sorrow.

This is the ritual for generating the bodhimind resolve in the presence of a master.

If no master is present, then one simply visualizes that the buddhas and bodhisattvas of the ten directions come forth as witnesses, one makes offerings to them, and then proceeds with the same liturgy as above. However, in this latter case one omits the words, "O spiritual master, grant me your attention."

Otherwise, the steps of taking refuge and generating the bodhimind resolve are much the same (whether or not there is a master present to lead the ritual).

(3) The Concluding Procedures
As before, the master of the ritual here reiterates the advice concomitant with having accepted the aspirational bodhimind. Whether or not one utilizes the above ritual to generate aspirational bodhimind, the thought to achieve full enlightenment in order to benefit all sentient beings, (or whether one generates this resolve in some other manner, such as being directly inspired by a living bodhisattva, generating it spontaneously in meditation, etc.), one's ability to maintain the advice of the aspirational bodhimind is the same. But certainly if one applies the above ritual and generates the thought to cultivate and never let weaken the bodhisattva attitude until enlightenment is achieved, one should maintain the advice and precepts of the aspirational bodhimind.

2. THE METHODS OF PROTECTING THE BODHISATTVA RESOLVE

This is taught under two headings: *(A)* cultivating the causes of not weakening the bodhisattva resolve in this lifetime, and *(B)* cultivating the causes of not becoming separated from it in future lives.

A) Not Weakening the Bodhisattva Resolve in this Lifetime

This is accomplished by means of four practices: *(1)* contemplating the beneficial effects of the bodhimind, which intensifies one's enthusiasm for the training; *(2)* constantly increasing the strength of the bodhimind, such as by generating it six times each day; *(3)* not abandoning the bodhimind toward any sentient being for any reason whatsoever; and *(4)* augmenting the collections of both merit and wisdom.

(1) The Beneficial Effects of the Bodhimind
The beneficial effects of the bodhimind are inconceivable. This point is expressed as follows in a scripture:

> When someone generates the bodhimind, then instantly
> All living beings bound in the prisons of samsara
> Praise him as having become a child of the buddhas;
> And he becomes an object of worship to men and gods.

Those practitioners who generate the bodhimind become objects of respect of all beings of the world, including men and gods. From the viewpoint of lineage they immediately outshine both shravaka and pratyekabuddha practitioners. From that moment onward even small acts of goodness produce great results. One will no longer accumulate any karmic causes for rebirth in the lower realms, and any such karmic seeds created in the past will begin to lose their strength. All activities from this time on become karmic causes of rebirths in the higher realms, and the strength of any such karmic seeds created in the past increases from high to higher.

What is the merit of the bodhimind like? If it were to take form all of space would not be able to contain it. Its merit is greater than that created by filling the universe with the seven precious gems and offering them to the buddhas, for in the end, it brings the great benefit of peerless, complete enlightenment, the state of buddhahood itself. As is said in *The Sutra Requested by Subahu,*[57]

> Should the merit of the bodhimind
> Ever assume physical form,
> All the skies would be filled
> Yet more still would remain.

(2) Increasing the Strength of the Bodhimind
This involves two practices: (a) cultivating the methods that prevent one from relinquishing the bodhimind; and (b) cul-

tivating the methods that actually increase it.

a. The methods that prevent one from relinquishing the bodhimind
Having in the presence of the buddhas, bodhisattvas and spiritual master taken the vow to achieve enlightenment in order to benefit all sentient beings, do not thereafter relinquish this resolve due to intimidation on seeing the limitless number of beings, the coarseness of their ways, the limitless deeds that must be accomplished, the intensity and duration of those deeds, and so forth.

Do not be faint-hearted, thinking thoughts like, "How can I possibly conceive of taking responsibility for all sentient beings?" Recollect that relinquishing the bodhimind resolve has heavier karmic consequences than those incurred when a monk breaks one of his root vows; it leads to rebirth in the realms of misery. In this context a scripture states,

> (Relinquishing) the bodhimind resolve
> Is heavier than (for a monk to break) a root precept.

And also,

> It is said that if one had mentally decided
> To give away merely a small, common object
> But then one does not give it to anyone,
> This leads to rebirth as a hungry ghost.

> Thus if with pure thought we invite
> All sentient beings to a feast of the delights
> Of peerless enlightenment, and then we deceive them,
> How can we expect to achieve happiness ourselves?

Find strength in the thought, "How wonderful that I am able to cultivate the thought of enlightenment!" and do not let the bodhimind weaken within you, as is stressed again and again in numerous scriptures.

(b) Applying the methods for increasing the bodhimind
It is not enough simply to guard against degenerating the bod-

himind resolve. One should also strive to increase it in strength. For this it is advised to generate the bodhimind three times each day and three times each night.

There are a number of ways to do this, one of which is the rather elaborate ritual described above. However, if this is too long a liturgical practice for you it is sufficient just to visualize the buddhas and bodhisattvas of the ten directions, make offerings to them, and then recite the following verse:

> To the buddhas, the Dharma and the supreme
> community
> I turn for refuge until enlightenment is achieved.
> By my practice of the six perfections
> May buddhahood be gained for the sake of all.

(3) Not Abandoning the Bodhimind toward Anyone
Do not weaken the bodhimind resolve by excluding any particular individuals from your meditations on love and compassion simply because they have behaved unpleasantly toward you, thinking thoughts like "I will never do anything to help that person."

(4) Augmenting the Collections of Merit and Wisdom
This is accomplished by all the various methods discussed earlier, such as making offerings (to the buddhas and bodhisattvas, meditating on emptiness), etc.

B) Cultivating the Causes of Not Becoming Separated from the Bodhisattva Resolve in Future Lives

This is taught under two headings: *(1)* abandoning the four black dharmas, which cause a weakening of the bodhimind resolve; and *(2)* cultivating the four white dharmas, which prevent this weakening.

(1) Abandoning the Four Black Dharmas
These four are: deceiving holy beings such as one's ordination master, spiritual preceptor or meditation teacher by means of lying to them, etc.; causing regret in other practitioners, when regret is uncalled for; becoming angry at and speaking

badly about beings who have entered into the Great Way; and engaging in false and deceptive behavior with any sentient being whatsoever, by means such as pretending neediness in order to be given something.

(2) The Four White Dharmas to be Cultivated
These four are: abandoning lying to anyone whomsoever, even in jest; engaging in ways based on sincere intentions, free of hypocrisy; regarding the bodhisattva practitioners of the Great Way as being fully accomplished buddhas and resounding their praises throughout the ten directions; and determining to personally place the beings to be matured on the stage of peerless enlightenment.

3. THE METHODS OF RESTORING THE BODHIMIND RESOLVE

Some teachers claim that if one creates a black dharma which weakens the bodhimind resolve, or mentally gives up on any individual sentient being, or generates the thought that "I cannot work for the benefit of living beings," and if the length of a session does not pass, this is merely the cause of a slight weakening of the bodhimind resolve. As the bodhimind has not actually been relinquished, there is no need to engage the ritual for generating it again. Only if a complete session has passed is it relinquished and is it therefore necessary to perform the ritual.

But in our tradition the bodhimind resolve is said to have been relinquished (not on the basis of these black dharmas) but the moment one experiences the thought, "I cannot work for the benefit of living beings." Thus the ritual to take the bodhimind resolve should be performed at that point.

As for the four black dharmas that cause a weakening of the bodhisattva spirit, they are not causes of relinquishing the bodhimind resolve in this life. Rather, they are causes for us to be separated from it in future lives. Nonetheless they should be avoided from this very moment.

II. CULTIVATING THE ULTIMATE BODHIMIND

The root text states,

When proficiency is attained,
Teach the secret (methods).

As said above, when the trainee has achieved stability in the trainings of the conventional bodhimind, he/she should be taught the methods of meditating upon emptiness, a subject held secret from those who grasp at inherent existence. He/she should then practice those meditations.

How does one meditate on emptiness? This can be studied in detail from any of the manuals known as "guidelines to the middle view."[58] The root text points out the essence of the techniques:

Consider how all phenomena are like dreams,
And examine the nature of unborn awareness.
The opponent is free on its own ground.
Place the essence of the path
In the sphere of the foundation of all.

Although the external objects such as mountains, houses, men, women and so forth appear to truly exist, in fact they do not. They are like the mountains, houses and people seen in a dream.

You may accept that external objects have no true existence, yet feel that the mind apprehending those objects does truly exist. When we examine the nature of awareness we soon see that it too lacks true existence, for it was never born in the ultimate sense. Neither self nor others nor both are produced without their respective causes (and thus they are dependent, and not 'ultimate' or 'independent' phenomena).

Perhaps you can see how both objects and consciousness are not truly existent, but feel that the opponent force, the wisdom that perceives the non-true existence of objects and consciousness, itself truly exists.

This too is without real status, for both objects and consciousness have been seen to lack true existence; and there is no phenomenon, including any opponent force, that is not encompassed within the twofold heading of 'objects and consciousness,' which would not be subsumed under one of these two categories. When this is understood, the mind that grasps at the true existence of the opponents is liberated on its own ground.

Where should one place the essence of one's practice? It should be placed on the foundation of all, the sphere of emptiness. The reason that emptiness is called 'the foundation of all' is that it is the foundation of everything in samsara and nirvana. Those who do not understand emptiness continue to wander in cyclic existence; those who understand it become free from cyclic existence.

Some scholars claim that this line refers to establishing the nature of the path on the *alaya vijnana*, or 'foundational consciousness' (literally, 'consciousness as the foundation of all'). The concept, borrowed from the Mind Only school of Indian Buddhist thought, is that there exists an 'eighth consciousness' that is different from any of the generally accepted six consciousnesses (i.e., the five sensory consciousnesses plus nonsensory mental experience). In their scheme of things, the seventh consciousness is a distorting conceptual mental factor, and thus is to be transcended.

However, there are philosophical problems associated with interpreting this line of the root text in such a manner. Firstly, their 'foundational consciousness' could not be generated in the nature of the path. Those who accept the existence of this 'foundational consciousness' assert that (in the threefold classification of phenomena into positive, negative and unspecified) it is an unspecified phenomenon; however, they classify the path as an exclusively positive phenomena.

Secondly, the apprehension of the path cannot be linked to the foundational consciousness; for the conventional level of reality does not appear within the framework of the apprehension of the path which is in the process of perceiving emptiness.

The root text then states,

> **In the post-meditation periods,**
> **Be like an illusory being.**

In those times when you have arisen from your meditation cushion, and consciousness and its objects seem to truly exist, meditate on the thought, "They seem to exist, yet they are like an illusion and like things seen in a dream."

Point Three: Transforming Negative Conditions into Aids on the Path

Transforming negative circumstances into limbs of enlightenment is taught under two headings: (I) doing so by means of focusing one's contemplation on the conventional bodhimind; and (II) doing so by means of focusing one's contemplation on the ultimate bodhimind.

I. FOCUSING CONTEMPLATION ON THE CONVENTIONAL BODHIMIND

Here the root text advises us,

Place all the blame upon one thing alone;
And meditate upon kindness for all.

Whenever any external hardships manifest, such as unprovoked aggression from humans, non-humans, malicious forces and so forth, or internal hardships such as illness, distorted emotions and so forth, do not place the blame on others. Rather, place it squarely on the self-cherishing attitude.

Think to yourself, "This self-cherishing attitude has caused me to experience countless sufferings since beginningless time. Even now it continues to draw me into limitless suffering and unpleasantness. And if I do not transcend it, it will continue to bring me misery without end. I should therefore make every possible effort to transcend it.''

Concerning any living beings who bring you hardship you should contemplate as follows:

''In my countless previous incarnations since time without beginning every single living being has served as a mother to me, not only once but again and again. On those occasions she brought me all the benefits that a mother brings to a child, and showed me the great kindness of protecting me from all that could bring me harm.

''Especially, this person now bringing me hardship has served as a mother to me in many incarnations since beginningless time, not only once but again and again. On those occasions she brought me all the benefits that a mother brings to a child, and showed me the great kindness of protecting me from all that could bring me harm.

''In her efforts to protect me she entered into much negative activity of body, speech and mind, and as a result even now she continues to experience the karmic fruit of that as frustration and suffering.

''Moreover, at the present moment she is unable to appreciate the intimacy of our karmic relationship due to the confusion created by birth, transmigration and rebirth. And inspired by my negative karma she comes now to harm me, by which she generates further negative karmic causes for her own future suffering. My heart goes out to her.

''May this unfortunate being have every happiness and be free from every misery. For this reason I will achieve enlightenment. And in my effort to achieve enlightenment this aggressor is a wonderful assistant, helping me to meditate on love, compassion and the bodhimind.''

Contemplating in this way, develop the mind that not only is not displeased with hardships, but actually finds joy in them.

II. FOCUSING CONTEMPLATION ON THE ULTIMATE BODHIMIND

The method of transforming negative circumstances into limbs of enlightenment by means of meditating upon the ultimate bodhimind proceeds as follows.

When external hardships from humans or non-humans arise, or internal hardships such as illness or afflicted emotions, reflect to yourself, "These things only appear to me due to the forces of my confusion. In fact they have no true existence." Investigate the situation deeply and ask how the event is produced in the beginning, how it resides in the middle, and how it ceases to exist in the end.

The reality of how in the beginning it was not truly produced from anything is the Unborn Truth Body (Skt., *Dharmakaya*). In the beginning not produced from anything, in the end it has no cause to cease to exist; this reality is the Unceasing Beatific Body (Skt., *Sambhogakaya*). The reality of non-creation and therefore non-cessation indicate the reality of non-abiding; this is the Non-Abiding Emanation Body (Skt., *Nirmanakaya*). This separation from birth, abiding and cessation is the Essence Body (Skt., *Svabhavikakaya*).

Meditate in this way on how all phenomena, especially the harm, the harmer and the harmed, are all without true existence. This meditation provides supreme protection from all harm. In this context a tantric scripture states,

> Awareness of emptiness is the supreme protector;
> With it, no other protection is needed.

And also,

> When one meditates on emptiness,
> Even the Lord of Death gains no entry.

Even meditating without a correct understanding of emptiness, and simply focusing the attention on nothingness, causes one to become less visible to those who cause harm. Concerning the above teaching the root text says,

> **Meditate that all confused appearances**
> **Are the four pristine *Buddhakayas*.**
> **Emptiness is the supreme protector.**

Point Four: The Doctrine of a Practice for One Lifetime

The doctrine of collecting all essential practices together and arranging them into a format for systematic and effective practice in one lifetime is given as follows in the root text:

Apply yourself to the five powers.

In other words, all practices should be linked to the five powers: *(1)* the power of the white seed, *(2)* the power of resolve, *(3)* the power of transcendence, *(4)* the power of familiarity, and *(5)* the power of aspiration.

(1) The Power of the White Seed
Here all creative energy generated by means of the body, speech and mind is dedicated to the goal that whatever levels of the two bodhiminds have not yet been generated may be generated; and that whatever levels of the two bodhiminds have been achieved may not become weakened or lost.

(2) The Power of Resolve
One projects the following resolve: "From now until enlightenment is attained may all sentient beings abide in happiness. May all sentient beings be free from suffering. For the benefit of all beings I myself will achieve the sublime state of perfect buddhahood."

Also think, "This self-cherishing attitude is the source of all suffering and unpleasantness. I shall transcend it."

(3) The Power of Transcendence
One cultivates the attitude, "Since beginningless time this self-cherishing attitude has caused me to experience limitless suffering. And it will continue to do so for as long as I have not transcended it."

Because of the influence of self-cherishing, many of the practitioners famed for their learning, gentleness, meditational endeavor and knowledge nonetheless remain prone to the delusions.

Consequently they harbor feelings of jealousy for those more advanced than themselves, disrespect for those less advanced, and competitiveness with those on the same level.

As a result, no matter how much they apply themselves to the Dharma methods they do not seem to come any closer to the spirit of liberation. They just end up walking around thinking their head rises a bit above that of everyone else, that they cover more territory than others, and that they are somehow separate from everyone else. Consequently wherever they go they receive little welcome; and no matter whom they go with, they always seem to encounter ill-will and conflict.

Determine therefore, "I will transcend this self-cherishing habit."

(4) The Power of Familiarity
Cultivating this power means meditating constantly on the two bodhiminds by means of the preliminaries, the actual methods, and the concluding processes, as explained earlier.

(5) The Power of Aspiration
This includes activities like making offerings to the Three Jewels and performing rituals to the Dharma protectors, and then offering the prayer, "In this life, at death, in the *bardo*,[59] in the next life and in all future reincarnations may the forces of the two bodhiminds not become weakened within me, but may they manifest with an ever-increasing strength. Should any difficult circumstances or hardships arise, may I take these

as friends in the cultivation of the two bodhiminds. May I always remain in touch with the Mahayana masters who teach this sublime path." Offer this aspiration at the conclusion of every spiritual activity.

How should the practitioner of this Mahayana lojong system deal with the advent of death? He/she should apply the Mahayana oral tradition method of applying the five forces. Here the root text states,

> **The Mahayana oral tradition for transference**
> **Is to cherish the path of the five forces.**

The names of the five are the same as with the five forces explained above, although the order and the interpretation are somewhat different.

Here the order of the five is as follows: *(1)* the power of the white seed, *(2)* the power of aspiration, *(3)* the power of transcendence, *(4)* the power of resolve, and *(5)* the power of familiarity. These are explained as follows.

(1) The Power of the White Seed
When the time of death has drawn near you should distribute wealth and possessions to wholesome causes. Then recollect and purify any gross negative actions created during your lifetime. Meditate upon refuge in the Three Jewels, give rise to thoughts of the altruistic bodhimind, and then reaffirm your commitment to the spiritual goals and values that you had cultivated during life.

(2) The Power of Aspiration
The second force is applied in the same manner as was explained earlier.

(3) The Power of Transcendence
To invoke the power of transcendence one reflects on the thought, "From beginningless time this self-cherishing attitude has brought me only suffering. It has generated only frustration and discomfort. And if I do not now transcend it, it will continue to bring sorrow and pain. I should remain free from all attachment to body and mind, and transcend this

enemy self-cherishing.''

(4) The Power of Resolve
Here the power of resolve is activated by reflecting on the thought, ''From now on I will meditate constantly on the two bodhiminds. Then in the *bardo* I will realize the clear light of mind and transform it into the Truth Body (Skt., *Dharmakaya*) of buddhahood, and for the benefit of others will spontaneously manifest in the sublime Form Body (Skt., *Rupakaya*) of a buddha.

(5) The Power of Familiarity
As the actual moment of death draws near lie down on your right side, with your right arm folded beside your body. Block your right nostril by pressing on the side of it with your right ring finger, thus causing the breath to pass through the left nostril. Without any thoughts of attachment to your body, etc., remain unintimidated by the approaching presence of death, like a son joyfully returning to his father's house after an absence of many years. Place the mind on the coming and going of the breath, and meditate in accordance with the lojong tradition of 'sending and receiving.' Visualize that as you exhale you send out joy and happiness to all sentient beings, and as you inhale you take from them all their frustration and pain.

Next imagine that the world and its inhabitants all dissolve into nothingness. Meditate on how all phenomena are without true existence; and especially on how birth and death are not truly existent. Then recollect how, even though not a single phenomenon truly exists, the sentient beings nonetheless grasp at all things as true and consequently experience suffering. Generate a sense of compassion for them, and meditate in accordance with the technique of 'sending and receiving.'

Pass away in the sphere of this meditation on compassion and wisdom combined.

Point Five: The Measure to Which the Mind Has Been Trained

The root text states,

All Dharmas condense into one intent.
(To measure your spiritual development,)
Hold to the chief of the two witnesses.

As said here, all teachings of the enlightened beings have but one purpose: to tame ego-grasping, the habit of reifying a truly existent self. It is the extent to which our so-called Dharma practice is curing us of ego-grasping that determines whether or not our training is maturing, whether or not we are really practicing the Dharma. When our study and application have become a remedy to ego-grasping, it has achieved at least a basic degree of maturity.

What witness can discern the extent to which our ego-grasping has been tamed? Of course other sentient beings can serve as a witness to our progress, and they can perceive some signs concerning our spiritual development. But they are not the principal witness, for they cannot know our thoughts. It is possible that they may over-estimate us merely because some of our mannerisms seem agreeable to them.

We are our own best witness. All we have to do is to look

inside ourselves and check to see if our ego-grasping is big or small.

Another basic factor to examine in order to determine the level of one's progress is given as follows in the root text:

The mind constantly relies upon joy alone.

The real sign of maturity in the training is one's inner joy. When one naturally regards any obstacles and unpleasantness that arise as friends come to help in the development of the two bodhiminds, and is able to do this with a mind that does not become diverted from a stream of constant joy, maturity in the training has been achieved. The root text states,

If there is ability even when distracted,
This too is a sign of progress.

An accomplished horse rider can race around without being thrown from his mount by any sudden movements that may occur. Similarly, when challenges come to us from unexpected quarters, hardships such as aggression, insults, accusations and humiliating encounters, if we are able to take them as friends come to help us in the development of the two bodhiminds this is a sign that progress has being made.

The root text states,

The measure of the training is read from its reverse.

The measure to which progress has been made along this path is the reverse of the intensity of the manifestations of those factors that are contradictory to the nature of the path. For example, the measure of the success of one's meditations upon the preciousness of human life adorned with the freedoms and endowments is the opposite of one's lack of aspiration and effort to take the spiritual essence of the opportunity provided by this extraordinary incarnation.

Similarly, the measure of one's training in the meditations upon emptiness can be determined by calculating the opposite of the level to which grasping at true existence manifests.

And what are the unmistaken signs of having fully trained the mind on this path? The root text states,

There are five great signs of accomplishment.

These five are as follows: one becomes a great bodhisattva, who through the lojong training is enabled to take any challenges and unpleasantness that arise in such a way that one's meditation upon the two bodhiminds is not weakened; one becomes a great master of self-discipline who, having ascertained the coarse and subtle levels of the nature of the karmic laws of cause and effect, protects oneself against becoming stained by even minor transgressions of the trainings; one becomes a great ascetic, able to accept with patience whatever hardships and unpleasant circumstances arise; one becomes a great practitioner, whose body, speech and mind are constantly focused on the spiritual path; and one becomes a great yogi, whose mind has become linked to the principal sentiment expressed by all the enlightenment teachings.

What are the means of producing these signs? The root text states,

The supreme method of four applications
Is superior to any other excellence.

To give rise to these signs one should engage the method possessing the four applications.

The first of these is to try to practice the Dharma in all circumstances. No matter what hardships or challenges arise the mind should be kept focused on Dharma practice, with the intent to increase the intensity of today's practice beyond that of yesterday, and that of this evening beyond that of this morning.

The second application is that, as the above is being cultivated, one applies oneself in thought to meditation upon the two bodhiminds, and in action to the various means of accumulation and purification.

Thirdly, whenever one experiences joy because of favorable conditions having ripened, and when the thought aspiring to that joy arises, one recollects how all other sentient beings also aspire to experience only happiness. Meditate on giving your own joy to all sentient beings. Imagine that all beings are placed in happiness. This aspiration to happiness is a signal that one should apply oneself to wholesome ways, the cause of all well-being. Thus the third application focuses on accumulating positive karmic energy.

Fourthly, this aspiration to experience only happiness and not to experience suffering or pain is a signal that we should transcend negative karma, the cause of all misery, and should purify the mind of negative karmic seeds by means of the four opponent forces.[60]

When any suffering or hardship arises within our continuum we should recollect how all other sentient beings similarly do not want suffering. Meditate on taking upon yourself the suffering of all sentient beings, and visualize that they become freed from it.

Unwanted suffering is a signal that we should strive to transcend negative karmic activity and should purify the mind of karmic seeds by means of the four opponent forces. It is also a signal that, as we wish to dwell in happiness, we should apply ourselves to the methods that accomplish goodness, the cause of happiness, and should strive at accumulation of wholesome spiritual power.

This method of training the mind on the path to enlightenment is especially exalted, for it enables the practitioner to take any sufferings and hardships that arise as friends in the development of the two bodhiminds.

Point Six: The Commitments of This Mind Training System

The root text states,

Constantly train in the three general points.

These are *(1)* not to contradict the general lojong sentiment, *(2)* not to use the lojong tradition for vain purposes, and *(3)* not to give the lojong teaching a prejudiced application.

The first of these is not to ignore aspects of the lojong teaching because of holding wrong attitudes such as, "I can meditate upon the lojong teachings and that is all I need to do. There is no need for me to engage in the other trainings, such as making prostrations, circumambulating holy images or monuments, reciting scriptures and mantras, etc."

The second point is never to contradict the sentiment of the lojong teaching when engaged in the various levels and aspects of training, from meditation on refuge up to the esoteric yogas of the highest tantras.

The third point is not to give the lojong teaching a prejudiced application. An example of a prejudiced application is to practice forbearance with the harms caused by non-humans, but not to do so with those caused by humans; or to practice forbearance with harms caused by humans, but not with those caused by non-humans. Another example is to treat great people with respect, but to be condescending toward people in lesser states. Or to show love and compassion to some beings, but aversion to others. Train the mind so as not to go in these prejudiced directions.

Concerning the next precept the root text states,

Meditate on the three unmitigated qualities.

The first of these is unmitigated respected for the spiritual teacher. One's teacher is the root of one's progress on the Mahayana path, so meditate on the recognition of him as being an actual buddha.

Secondly, this lojong tradition is the very quintessence of the Mahayana path. In the practice of it, meditate with unmitigated joy.

Thirdly, one should meditate with unmitigated mindfulness on maintaining the precepts and commitments that have been adopted.

The root text:

Train in the three difficult practices.

When a distorting emotion arises, it is difficult to respond by meeting it with its specific opponent meditation. Even when the specific opponent is applied, it is difficult to turn back the deluded emotional force. Thirdly, even if we are able to turn away the delusion on a given occasion, it is difficult to cause it to be unable to arise again in the future.

Apply the force of familiarity to help you train in these three difficult practices.

The root text:

Cultivate the three principal causes.

Although the factors that act as causes in the accomplishment of buddhahood are limitless, there are three principal ones.

The first of these is the internal condition of the capacity to generate realization of the spiritual teachings within one's mindstream, from the contemplation of the preciousness and rarity of having found a human incarnation blessed with the freedoms and endowments, up to the meditations on the meaning of emptiness, just as taught by the guru. The second and third are external: being cared for by a qualified spiritual master; and having the physical necessities of practice, such as food, clothing and shelter.

Having all three conditions is a principal cause (i.e., three principal causes) of enlightenment. You should check to see whether or not they are present within your stream of being. If they are, put them to good use by making a sincere effort to accomplish buddhahood.

If not all of them are present, consider how there are limitless other sentient beings like you who do not have the complete causes of buddhahood. Engage the 'sending and receiving' meditation, taking from them all their negative karma and suffering. Imagine that in this way they become separated from all misery, and they achieve all conditions conducive to attaining buddhahood.

The root text:

Possess the three inseparables.

The first of these is to be inseparable from the spiritual activities of the body, such as showing respect to the teacher, offering physical prostrations, making circumambulations, etc. The second is to be inseparable from the spiritual activities of speech, such as chanting the scriptures, reciting mantras, offering verses of praise to the buddhas, and so forth. The third is to be inseparable from the spiritual activities of the mind, such as meditating on the two bodhiminds, etc.

The root text:

Do not speak about weakened limbs.

Perhaps we know people who, from the viewpoint of worldly beings, suffer from physical handicaps such as having only one eye or being deaf, or who suffer from failures in spiritual practice, or who appear as immoral, and so forth. Do not make these an object of your mockery, for to do so generates discomfort in the minds of the recipients of your poor wit, and it also creates hindrances to your own meditation on lojong. The root text:

Do not judge others.

Do not say things about others, such as, "That person is utterly unacceptable company." From our side we have undertaken to cultivate the lojong tradition; if we allow ourselves to pick out faults in others, we contradict the lojong trainings. There is no need to observe shortcomings in others, and certainly there is no spiritual benefit in speaking of others' faults.

Should you allow yourself to become dominated by the thought wishing to see only faults in others, or wishing to speak about others' faults, there is no way to use the occasion as a method for abiding in the lojong training.

Thus do not observe nor speak about faults of others in general, nor of Dharma practitioners and those on the Great Way in particular. To do so has many unpleasant ripening effects; it cuts off the root of one's meritorious energy and creates the seeds of a lower rebirth. Should you accidentally notice a shortcoming in someone, think to yourself, "This appearance is a reflection of my own impure mind. How can that person possibly have such a fault!"

The root text:

Engage two practices:
One at the beginning and one at the end.

When you wake up in the morning make firm the thought, "Today I will not allow any of my activities to become stained by self-cherishing. I will remain inseparable from the thought of cherishing others and from the two bodhiminds." Then hold to this resolve with mindfulness and alertness.

Secondly, before you go to bed at night reflect back on your activities of the day and check to see whether or not they were stained by fallacious, un-Dharmic factors.

If it seems that they were, you should contemplate the thought, "Today I have not used this precious human life meaningfully. I am like the person who inflicts harm upon himself." Generate regret and purify the failing by means of applying the four opponent forces.

If they were not tainted by self-cherishing, meditate joyfully on the thought, "Today my life has been meaningful. This human incarnation has brought about some progress on the spiritual path."

Offer the prayer, "From now on throughout this life, and throughout all my future lives, may I not become separated from meditation upon the two bodhiminds."

The root text:

Maintain patience for whichever of the two arises.

Should one suddenly experience pleasing events, such as admiration from others, possessions, wealth, praise, fame and so forth, do not react with pride. Instead, meditate on how these conditions are impermanent and essenceless, like things enjoyed in a dream, and take them as factors supportive of your Dharma practice.

Alternatively, should you experience events that make you feel so low that it seems like even water cannot run under you, do not think that you are alone in your hardships. Instead, practice the meditation of 'sending and receiving,' visualizing that you take upon yourself the hardships of all other beings. Think to yourself, "In comparison to the difference between the experiences of the upper and lower realms of samsara, the difference between pleasure and pain in this life is insignificant. I should simply continue my practice of the holy Dharma. That will make this precious human incarnation that I have achieved most meaningful." Contemplating in this way, take the negative experience as an aid facilitating your accomplishment of the enlightenment path.

The root text:

When both are present, take all (upon yourself).

Whenever any of the afflicted emotions or delusions arise within your mindstream, such as craving, anger, jealousy or pride, engage the meditation of 'sending and receiving,' visualizing that you take upon yourself the afflicted emotions and delusions of all sentient beings. Imagine that in this way all beings are freed from these negative factors.

Similarly whenever suffering or unpleasantness arise within you, meditate that by means of it you take upon yourself the suffering and hardships of all other beings. Imagine that thus all beings are freed from misery.

The root text:

Guard two things like you would your life.

By not guarding one's spiritual commitments, all the happiness of this and future lives is obstructed. Therefore one should protect the general precepts of Dharma practice, and especially the precepts of this lojong tradition, as one would one's life.

The general precepts of Dharma practice are of two types: those which one has resolved to cultivate; and the precepts of the guru. One should guard the former of these with one's life. As for the latter, no matter what the qualifications of one's teacher it is unadvisable to break the precepts related to him; for to do so renders it impossible in the future to attain the realizations that depend upon the guru. Hence this precept too should be guarded with one's life.

Concerning the special precepts of this lojong tradition (that are listed here), they too should be maintained with great care. For example, other than as a helpful, discrete reminder, one should never speak of faults or failings in others.

The root text:

Avoid partiality.

Although the mental capacity, nature and quality of ordinary beings are only partially developed, we should not be partial in our practice of the six perfections, our application to the activities of study, contemplation and meditation, and our cultivation of the ten ways of Dharma. Some of these things we can actually do, and others we can perhaps only visualize doing.

Also, concerning the sentient beings who are the objects of our practice, we should train without being partial toward beings on high and those on lesser stages of development. Show an equal respect to all.

The root text:

Constantly practice on special cases.

We should in general train our mind using all sentient beings as the object; but in particular we should show special care with the five following types of people: close companions; competitors who have harmed us; those who, even though we have not harmed them, cause harm to us; those who, even though they haven't harmed us, seem unpleasant and repulsive to us; and those who have brought us great benefits, such as our spiritual teachers, parents and so forth. With the first four of these groups there is a strong danger that we could mistake the training by mixing the afflicted emotions into our dealings with them; as for the fifth category, we should be especially careful because here a small mistake can have heavy ripening karmic results due to the great kindnesses that these people have shown to us. These are special cases and we should meditate with special intensity when in their company.

The root text:

Train in the easy practice.

Some people think, "It simply is not possible for me now to take upon myself the suffering and negative karma of others, nor to give them my happiness or merit." However, there is no need to engage in austerities of body and speech. It is enough simply to train in the mind, by meditating and thus transforming our perspective. The question of creating hardships for ourselves through making such personal sacrifices therefore does not arise. The fault of not being able to meditate upon 'sending and receiving' does not exist.

The root text:

Purify the most coarse factor first.

We should constantly examine our mind to see what delusion or afflicted emotion is the strongest within us, and what is the most immediately detrimental to our spiritual growth. Whatever is the most coarse should be purified first.

The root text:

Avoid yet practice getting tough.

There is no need to get tough with humans or non-humans; in fact, to do so is harmful to us both conventionally and spiritually.

With what should we get tough? With the self-cherishing attitude, which is the root of all our suffering. We should make this the target of our every spiritual endeavor.

The root text:

Avoid food mixed with poison.

Wholesome food supports our body and life; but should poison become mixed into it, this same food then has the reverse effect. Similarly, spiritual practice is the life force supporting higher being and final goodness; yet when we mix the poison of self-cherishing into our practice it harms our capacity to achieve higher being and final goodness. Therefore avoid mixing the poison of self-cherishing into the food of spiritual practice.

The root text:

Do not depend upon soft treatment.

Some practitioners are able to practice love and compassion toward pleasant beings, but toward those who cause hardships they harbor resentment. We should not be like that. Such behavior is not worthy of someone training in accordance with the shravaka vehicle, let alone someone aspiring to the bodhisattva path.

The root text:

Do not plan revenge.

Sometimes when someone harms us we do not immediately express our resentment, but instead harbor thoughts to seek revenge later. Avoid all thoughts of revenge.

The root text:

Do not be cunning.

When you see someone else in possession of something that you crave for yourself, do not use deceptive means in order to acquire it.
The root text:

Do not put the load of a *dzo* on a bullock.[61]

For example, if there is some task or hardship that is about to fall on either you or someone else, do not use deceptive and cunning means in order to divert it from you to the other person.
The root text:

Do not rejoice in sorrow.

We should not take causes of other people's sorrow as causes of our own happiness. For example, should a competitor die we should not rejoice in the thought that his death will benefit our own position. Or if a friend or relative dies we should not rejoice in the fact that as a consequence we will receive some of his possessions. Or should a patron die we should not rejoice in the thought that we will inherit something from him. Never take the suffering of others as limbs of your own happiness.
The root text:

Do not engage in wrong methods of healing.

Sometimes in this world when a cherished person becomes ill his family or friends perform or commission a faith healer to perform any of the various healing rituals, such as *shi-dra* (Shi-gra) or *lu-tang-wa* (gLud-gtong-ba), in order that the person may not die. However, we should not use the lojong meditations as methods to cure ourself of illness. This is not their purpose or function.
The root text:

Avoid the mistaken attitudes.

That is to say, we should avoid the six mistaken attitudes, and cultivate the six unmistaken ones. The six mistaken attitudes are as follows:

The first is mistaken priorities. This means not dedicating our energy to practicing the Dharma in accordance with the thought of the enlightened beings, but instead dedicating it to achieving mere worldly success.

Next is mistaken patience. Instead of having patience with the hardships encountered in the practice of the enlightenment path, we have it for the hardships encountered in the activities of outdoing competitors and assisting friends.

The third factor is mistaken taste. Here we have no taste for spiritual activities, such as study, contemplation and meditation, the endeavors that lead to higher being and enlightenment, yet we have a taste for worldly activities and indulgence.

The fourth is mistaken compassion. This occurs when, instead of feeling compassion for prosperous people who achieved their success by indulging in negative activity, the karmic cause of future misery, we feel it for Dharma practitioners and yogis who perhaps lack adequate food, clothing or shelter due to the sacrifices they have made to pursue the spiritual path.

Next is mistaken encouragement. That is, although one has resolved to liberate all sentient beings from suffering, yet instead of encouraging those who look to us for advice to make efforts to accomplish the practice of the spiritual path we encourage them to make efforts to gain worldly advancement and prosperity.

Finally, mistaken rejoicing occurs when, instead of rejoicing in the spiritual goodness of oneself and others, we rejoice in any misery that befalls those who have caused us harm.

The root text:

Do not strike sensitive areas.

That is to say, do not speak of the failings and faults of others when in a public place.

The root text:

Do not turn a god into a devil.

When one relies upon and propitiates the worldly gods they can bring us great benefits and can protect us from harm. However, if later we ignore them or treat them with disrespect they can also bring us many problems. This is known as turning a god into a ghost.

Similarly, our practice of the lojong tradition is meant to bring us the benefits of happiness and enlightenment by eliminating the afflictive emotions from within us. Should it be applied in such a way that all it does is increase the afflictive emotions of pride, arrogance, self-cherishing and so on, this is like turning a god into a devil. Avoid allowing your practice to develop in this direction.

The root text:

Do not be inconsistent.

We should not be inconsistent in our behavior toward others, showing various expressions of pleasure and displeasure with ostensibly good and bad things done by them. It is better to react consistently with warmth and humor. Otherwise we cause anxiety in the minds of others.

Similarly one should not be inconsistent in one's application to the meditational trainings, sometimes practicing intensely and at other times hardly practicing at all. An inconsistent endeavor lacks the power to induce attainment.

The root text:

Do not be unbalanced.

In other words, do not be one-sided in the twofold training of wisdom and activity. We should appreciate how not even the tiniest particle of matter has inherent existence, yet on the conventional level of truth all actions have karmic validity.

Practice this path of the inseparable nature of the view (of emptiness) and the various activities without stressing one to the detriment of the other.

The root text:

Train in both the main body and the limbs.

Take, for instance, the trainings in the conventional bodhimind. Here the preliminary meditations, such as the contemplation of the preciousness and rarity of having acquired a human incarnation blessed by the freedoms and endowments, serve as the limb of preparation; the meditations on interwoven 'sending and receiving' are the main body of the practice; and then the limb of concluding procedures is comprised of the meditations on the emptiness of inherent existence of all phenomena, as well as the practice of sealing the endeavor with the dedication of merit and the offering of spiritual aspirations.

Similarly, in the trainings in the ultimate bodhimind the limb of preparation is comprised of all the meditations up to and including those on the conventional bodhimind. The actual body of the practice is the meditation on emptiness, and the limb of concluding procedures is comprised of practices such as generosity, etc.

The root text:

Practice without bias toward the objects;
Embrace everything and cherish all from the heart.

We should train in the lojong methods without fear of the challenges presented by sentient and insentient phenomena alike. Moreover, in this endeavor we should be inspired and guided by the two bodhiminds.

Our practice should not be like the way a handful of roasted barley flour thrown into a pot of beer merely floats on the top. Our respect for others should arise from within the innermost depths of our being.

Point Seven:
Advice to Lojong Practitioners

The root text states,

Practice all yogas in one manner.

A tantric practitioner utilizes yogic methods such as the yoga of washing, the yoga of eating, the yoga of sleeping, and so forth. In this lojong system the practitioner turns all yogas toward the one activity of meditation on the two bodhiminds.
The root text:

Use all remedies in one manner.

No matter what sufferings or unpleasantness arise, meet them all with the one remedy of meditation upon the bodhimind.
The root text states,

Do not harbor resentment.

Should someone harm you in any way, do not dwell on thoughts such as, "He did this and this to me." Don't allow your mind to entertain negative mental images of others.
The root text:

Do not respond with arrogance.

That is to say, no matter what difficulties others may bring upon you, do not react with violence or with threatening words. The root text:

Do not wish for praise.

Even though we may not wish to receive an actual object or favor in return for a kindness we have shown to someone, yet we sometimes can find ourselves craving for the pleasure of hearing them speak about our beneficial act. Then when they don't speak about the incident we think, "It does not make the slightest difference whether I do good or bad to this person, for he does not even mention the beneficial things I've done for him." Avoid harboring such cravings for the sound of your own praise. The root text:

Do not become familiar with vanity.

That is to say, do not let the mind dwell on thoughts of what you have done for others. Just content yourself with the knowledge that the person has been benefited in some small way. That should be enough of a reward. Over our countless incarnations since beginningless time every sentient being has been a mother to us, not just once but again and again, and on those occasions has given all the benefits that a mother brings her offspring.

Moreover, if through our activity a sentient being has been brought closer to the ground of enlightenment, then our vow to benefit all beings has become somewhat fulfilled. There is no need to look back proudly; for at the time of undertaking the resolve to highest enlightenment we vowed in the presence of all the buddhas and bodhisattvas to bring happiness and liberation to all living beings. The root text:

Meditate in accordance with whatever occurs.

In times of happiness or hardship, whether in a city or in a meditational hermitage, and in general in all activities, whether moving, sitting standing or lying down, constantly

meditate on the lojong teaching.
The root text:

Do not rely upon external conditions.

Most Dharma practitioners rely upon being free from negative conditions, such as illness, etc., and rely upon having conducive conditions, such as sufficient food and clothing, etc.

But in this tradition the presence of negative factors and the absence of conducive conditions are simply taken within the scope of the lojong meditation.
The root text:

Crush all excuses.

Sometimes we may find ourself using excuses to validate our enmity toward others, such as "He did this and this." It is better to crush the inimical mind and instead meditate on cultivating a sense of love for all, that does not see some as near and others as far.
The root text:

Think deeply with insight and analysis.

Apply insight and analysis to observe the state of your mind and the forces of the afflicted emotions that course through it. Check to see what inner forces are presently the most obstructive to your spiritual growth, and then apply the meditative opponents to them.
The root text:

Practice with confidence.

When an afflicted emotion or delusion arises in the mind, do not hesitate to apply the counteractive meditations due to doubt, thinking self-defeating thoughts like, "Is this opponent force by itself sufficient to accomplish the task at hand?" Apply the various methods within the framework of the confidence that you are able to execute them effectively.
The root text:

Immediately accomplish what is important.

In the past we have taken countless rebirths in samsara, but these have largely been wasted on worldly purposes and have left us with nothing. We should use this precious human life that we have acquired as a tool for accomplishing what is important. As for just what is important: Within works that benefit this short life, or spiritual practice that benefits in ways more lasting, the latter is the more important. Within the two categories of theories of Dharma and the actual practice of it, the latter is the more important.

Finally, from within all the diverse Dharma practices that exist, the most important is the practice of meditation upon the two bodhiminds. It is this that we should make our foremost priority.

The root text:

Accomplish what is the most meaningful.

Activities such as building temples, creating religious statues and paintings, etc., are not always spiritually beneficial endeavors. Sometimes in our efforts in these directions we may disturb other beings; we may become removed from the practice of intense meditation; we may become involved with distracting people or become addicted to having human company; or our involvement in these activities may harm or even kill other living beings.

Well then, what is most meaningful? It is the inner spiritual activities, such as maintaining the spiritual commitments and precepts we have adopted; and cultivating our stream of being through the threefold application of hearing, contemplation and meditation. Take these up in order to be of maximum benefit to the world.

The root text:

Avoid all hopes of results.

The person who practices meditation in accordance with this lojong tradition will experience a vast array of temporary and lasting beneficial effects. Harmful forces and disruptive elements will cease of their own accord; one will come to be favored by men and gods alike; one will attain both prosperity and respect; in future lives one will achieve a high rebirth conducive to further training; and eventually one will attain the full power of final enlightenment.

But we should avoid having hopes or expectations for these things. Instead, dwell within the aspiration to achieve liberation and enlightenment for the benefit of all sentient beings, and meditate on the lojong technique of 'sending and receiving.'

The root text:

In future always wear the bodhisattva armor.

You may think, "If we should avoid all hopes for results, then there will be no stimulus for practicing the spiritual path."

The purpose of our practice should not be merely to benefit ourselves. Rather, we should constantly remind ourselves that over our countless past lives since beginningless time every sentient being has been a mother to us on one occasion or another, and not just once but again and again. In those lives they brought us all the benefits that a mother brings to her child, and protected us from all harm.

Generate love and compassion for all living beings in this way, and determine to accomplish buddhahood in order to be of greater benefit to the world. And as to accomplish the state of buddhahood one has to meditate on the two bodhiminds, cultivate the thought, "I will accomplish the practices of meditation upon the two bodhiminds."

Put on the bodhisattva armor of this thought six times every day.

The colophon [added by the original fifteenth-century compiler/editor of the First Dalai Lama's text]: This brief commentary to the Mahayana lojong [Tib., Theg-chen-blo-sbyong] tradition was written by the omniscient Gendun Druppa [Tib., dGe-'dun-grub-pa], an incarnation of the Bodhisattva Avalokiteshvara, embodiment of the knowledge and compassion of all the buddhas, with the thought to benefit the living beings of this degenerate age. Gendun Druppa composed it while living in Tashi Lhunpo Monastery [Tib., bKra-shi-lhun-po], a crown jewel adorning this world, a magic garden wherein all negative forces are transcended.

May it cause the precious enlightenment teachings to spread, to increase in strength and purity, and to remain for long in this world; and may it increase the happiness and freedom of living beings.

May spiritual energy, goodness and every auspicious sign manifest on earth. May living beings achieve inner peace, liberation and enlightenment.

Notes

TRANSLATOR'S INTRODUCTION

1. The most comprehensive study of the life and works of Atisha is that published by A. Chattopadhya and Lama Chinpa, *Atisha and Tibet* (Calcutta: R.D. Press, 1967). This is a highly academic historical analysis.

A second valuable work is Lama Drom Tonpa's traditional biography of Dipamkara Shrijnana, translated into English by Lama Thubten Kalsang et alia, entitled *Atisha* (Bangkok: The Social Science Association Press, 1974). This text has some detail on Atisha's voyage to Indonesia and his studies under Serlingpa.

Also, in conjunction with Ven. Doboom Tulku I compiled a small work on Atisha, entitled *Atisha and Tibetan Buddhism* (New Delhi: Tibet House, 1982). This small volume contains a translation of the short biography of Atisha found in the introductory section of Tsongkhapa's *Lam-rim-chen-mo*, as well as several translated verse works by Dipamkara. The edition was brought out on the 1,000th anniversary of Dipamkara's birth, which was celebrated in India as a national holiday.

2. A number of English translations of commentaries to the *Seven Points for Training the Mind* have previously appeared. The first of these was that of Jamgon Kongtrul (Tib., 'Jam-mgon-kong-sprul), translated by Ken MacLeod (Vancouver: Kargyu Kunkhyab Choling, 1976). In fact, Jamgon's text seems to have been largely a rewrite of an earlier Tibetan commentary by the renowned Tokmey

Zangpo (Tib., Thogs-med-bzang-po).

A modern oral commentary by the recently deceased Geshe Rabten appeared in 1977 in the collection *Advice from a Spiritual Friend*, translated by Gonzar Tulku and Brian Beresford (New Delhi: Wisdom Publications, 1977).

The third to appear was the shorter of the First Dalai Lama's two commentaries, included in my study of the life and works of that sage, *Selected Works of the Dalai Lama I: Bridging the Sutras and Tantras* (Ithaca, N.Y.: Snow Lion Publications, 1981).

In addition, my *Selected Works of the Dalai Lama VII: Songs of Spiritual Change* (Ithaca, N.Y.: Snow Lion Publications, 1982) is a collection of mystical songs and poems inspired by the Great Seventh's personal experiences of lojong meditation.

3. No major study of Indonesian Buddhist lineages surviving in Tibet has yet been made. Some years ago I had thought to undertake such a project myself, with the idea that it may cast some light on the significance and history of the wonderful Buddhist monuments at Borobudur.

Tibetan lineages coming from Indonesia were not limited to those brought by Atisha. Tibetan histories such as *The Blue Annals* translated by George Roerich (Calcutta: The Royal Asiatic Society, 1949), mention numerous other Tibetan teachers who made the journey to "The Golden Islands," or who studied with Indonesian masters in India, and subsequently brought their lineages to Tibet.

The writings of another of the First Dalai Lama's teachers, the controversial Bodong Chokley Namgyal (Tib., Bo-gdong-phyogs-las-rnam-rgyal), who was probably the most prolific author in human history, may offer further clues to Indonesia's lost Buddhist past.

4. For more on the teachers in the line of transmission of the early Kadampa lineage see *The Blue Annals*.

5. *Path of the Bodhisattva Warrior: Life and Teachings of the Thirteenth Dalai Lama* (Ithaca, New York: Snow Lion Publications, 1988).

6. To my knowledge, not yet available in English.

7. *Selected Works of the Dalai Lama I: Bridging the Sutras and Tantras* (Ithaca, New York: Snow Lion Publications, 1981).

8. *The Nine Ways of Bon* (Oxford University Press, 1967).

9. See *Tibet: A Dreamt of Image*, Jack Finnigan (New Delhi: Tibet House, 1986).

10. Stephen Batchelor, *The Tibet Guide* (London: Wisdom Publications, 1987).

11. Quoted here from *Bridging the Sutras and Tantras.*

TRAINING THE MIND IN THE GREAT WAY

1. Tib., Theg-chen-blo-sbyong; pronounced *tekchen lojong.*

2. It is said that in total Lama Atisha studied with more than fifty spiritual masters. Yet he always expressed the greatest appreciation for the three mentioned in this passage. In particular, he considered his Indonesian master Serlingpa to have been his closest and most important spiritual guide.

3. Tib., bDud-rtsi-snying-po; pronounced *dutsi nyingpo.*

4. This lama was the grand abbot of Nartang Monastery when the First Dalai Lama entered as a novice at the age of seven. He served as the presiding master for the youth's basic monastic ordination, and it was from him that the First Dalai Lama received the name Gendun Druppa, by which he was known throughout his life. From that time onward the abbot provided the young monk-scholar with material as well as spiritual support. In fact he became almost a second father to Gendun Druppa during these formative years.

5. Lama Chekhawa is mentioned by the Thirteenth Dalai Lama in the passage concerning the lojong lineage quoted above in the introduction. It was Chekhawa who, fearing for the survival of the tradition, first committed to paper the teaching of *Seven Points for Training the Mind.* See *The Blue Annals.*

6. *A Guide to the Bodhisattva Ways;* Tib., sPyod-'jug; Skt., *Bodhisattva-charya-avatara.* A number of English translations of this work are available, the most accurate (though not the most elegant) being that of Stephen Batchelor, *A Guide to the Bodhisattva's Way of Life,* published by the Library of Tibetan Works and Archives (Dharamsala: 1981).

7. This is the monastery established in 1409 by Lama Tsongkhapa, founder of the Gelukpa order. It came to be used as a model for the hundreds of Gelukpa monasteries that sprang up in the decades to follow.

8. It was in the Olkha Mountains that Lama Tsongkhapa had earlier done his five-year meditational retreat. It is said that during this retreat he and six of his eight attending disciples abstained from coarse food, using the powers of their meditation to survive

on only a handful of juniper berries each day.

9. Ganden Monastery originally had two departments, the 'Western Peak' and the 'Northern Peak.' Lama Namkha Palden was from the latter, known as Ganden Jangtse.

10. The shravakas and pratyekabuddhas are said to seek the solitary peace of individual nirvana, a complacent attainment surpassed by the "non-abiding" nirvana of the bodhisattva.

The bodhisattva attainment is "non-abiding," for it abides neither in samsara nor nirvana. As is so often said in the Mahayana scriptures, the bodhisattva's wisdom provides him liberation from samsara; yet his great compassion will not allow him to rest in the tranquility of nirvana.

11. Sometimes we see it said that the bodhisattva forgoes his own enlightenment in order to stay in the world and work for the welfare of the living beings. In fact this is not the case at all; on the contrary, the bodhisattva attempts to achieve enlightenment as quickly as possible in order to be of greater benefit to the living beings. This point is emphatically made by the First Dalai Lama later on in his commentary.

12. That is to say, the historical Buddha, who was born Siddhartha, became Gotama the Monk, and later achieved enlightenment to become a 'Buddha.' Shakyamuni literally means 'sage of the Shakya family.' Siddhartha's father was of the Shakya blood line. Thus after his enlightenment Gotama the Monk became known as Buddha Shakyamuni.

13. Ancient India saw considerable debate between these two principal trends of Buddhist thought. In Tibet, however, the conflict was avoided by regarding both trends as being different aspects of one person's practice: the former as an outer trend toward moderation and simplicity, and the latter as the heart and vision of great compassion.

14. That is to say, we must learn how to listen with openness to the spiritual master. But as the Fourteenth Dalai Lama points out in his commentary to *Essence of Refined Gold* (Ithaca, N.Y.: Snow Lion Publications, 1982), this does not mean that we should surrender our reason or critical intelligence in our dealings with the guru.

15. These represent the compassion, wisdom and power of enlightenment, respectively.

16. One repeats this mantra of consecration for each of the seven offerings, substituting for *ARGHAM* the names of the other offer-

ing substances: *PADYAM, PUSHPE, DHUPE, ALOKE, NAIVEDYA* and *SHABDA,* respectively. These are the substances symbolically placed in the seven offering bowls that Tibetans generally keep on their altars: the two cooling waters, and the objects of the five senses.

17. These four syllables symbolize the nearing, merging, uniting and becoming indivisible with the forces of transcendence.

18. This is the opening section of a liturgy known in Sanskrit as the *Mahayana-pranidana-raja,* or "King of Mahayana Aspirations." It is taken from the *Gandhavyuha-sutra,* which in turn is a section of the great Mahayana scripture known as the *Avatamsaka Sutra.*

19. This and most of the following quotes from Nagarjuna found in the preliminary section of the First Dalai Lama's commentary are taken from Nagarjuna's *Letter to a Friend* (Tib., *bShes-sbring,* Skt., *Suhrllekha*). This work is available in English as *Nagarjuna's Letter,* translated by Geshe Lobsang Tharchin and Artemus B. Engle (Dharamsala: Library of Tibetan Works and Archives, 1979).

20. *The Collected Sayings of the Buddha* (Tib., *'Ched-du-brjod-pai-tshoms,* Skt., *Udanavarga.*) English translation by Gareth Sparham, *The Tibetan Dhammapada* (New Delhi: Mahayana Publications, 1983).

21. *Draminyan* and *Dzambuling:* these are the Tibetan names for two of the legendary 'continents,' or worlds in which humans live, as derived from Indian mythology. The former is 'the northern continent,' a fabulous land of plenty, where the sun causes the sky to glimmer with an emerald hue; the latter is our planet earth, 'the southern planet,' where the sun causes the sky to appear as lapis blue.

22. Nagarjuna's *Letter to a Friend.*

23. *A Guide to the Bodhisattva Ways;* Skt., *Bodhisattva-charya-avatara;* Tib., *sPyod-'jug.*

24. Yojana: a measurement of armspans, approximately four miles.

25. *The Hundred and Fifty Praises;* Tib., *bsTod-pa-brgya-lnga-bcu-pa;* Skt., *Satapancashatka-stotra.*

26. *A Tapestry of Verse;* Tib., *sPel-mar-bsTod-pa;* Skt., *Mishraka-stotra.*

27. This phenomenon seems to manifest with some Tibetan lamas, especially those who do not speak English very well yet nonetheless teach in English. A case in point is Lama Tubten Zopa

Rinpoche, the lama from the Mt. Everest region of Nepal who was in charge of the search for the reincarnation of Lama Tubten Yeshe that led to the Spanish child now famed as Lama Osel Torres.

It is never easy to decide precisely what Lama Zopa is saying; everyone seems to hear something unique to their own karmic predispositions. A woman friend of mine once attended a Heruka initiation being given by Lama Zopa, and as the first day of the gathering ended Lama Zopa said something that she couldn't quite put together.

She asked a German sitting on her right, who whispered back, "He said we should all think like Heruka." Unconvinced, she asked the person sitting on her left. "He said that we should be back here tomorrow at two," came the reply.

It seems that the former had heard the most transcendental meaning; the latter had honed in on a more practical and mundane interpretation.

This anecdote encouraged my confidence as a translator of Tibetan classical texts. I rarely find passages with such divergent levels of meaning.

28. *The Chapter of the Truthful One;* Tib., *bDen-pa-poi-leu.* This text does not have a separate listing in the *Tengyur* catalogue. It is a small work included, I believe, in the collection known as *Atisha's One Hundred Little Dharmas* (Tib., *Jo-bo-chos-chung-brgya-rtsa*).

29. *In Praise of the Praiseworthy;* Tib., *bsNgag-os-bsngag-bstods;* Skt., *Devatishaya-stotra.*

30. *In Praise of the Superior One;* Tib., *Phags-bstod;* Skt., *Vishesa-stava.*

31. *The Summary;* Tib., *bsDud-pa;* Skt., *Prajnaparamitopadesha.* This and "the oral tradition" are mentioned several times by the First Dalai Lama. In fact this is probably not referring to an oral tradition as such, but to the contents of the text known as *Prajnaparamita-pindartha* (Tib., *Shes-phyin-man-ngag.*)

32. *The Sutra of Buddha's Passing;* Tib., *Mya-ngan-las-'das-pai-mdo;* Skt., *Maha-parinirvana-sutra.*

33. *The King of Absorptions Sutra;* Tib., *mDo-ting-'zin-rgyal-po;* Skt., *Samadhi-raja-sutra.*

34. *The Immortal Drumbeat;* Tib., *'Chi-med-rnga-sgrai-gzungs.* This is listed in the *Tengyur* catalogue, but no Sanskrit title is given.

35. *The Condensed Perfection of Wisdom Sutra;* Tib., *Phar-phyin-bsdus-pa;* Skt., *Paramita-samasa.*

36. *The Sayings on Mindfulness,* from *The Collected Sayings of the Buddha;* Tib., *'Ched-du-brjod-pai-tshoms;* Skt., *Udanavarga.*

37. Devaputra: one of the four main classes of *maras,* or harmful spirits.

38. *The Sutra Revealing the Four Dharmas;* Tib., *Chos-bshi-bstan-pai-mdo;* Skt., *Caturdharmaka-sutra.*

39. These aspects of karma and its fruit are discussed at length in *The Jewel Ornament of Liberation,* translated by Herbert V. Guenther (London: Rider & Co., 1959), pages 74-83.

40. *The Ornament of Mahayana Sutras;* Tib., *mDo-sde-rgyan;* Skt., *Mahayana-sutra-alamkara.*

Also *Sutra on the Perfection of Wisdom;* Tib., *Phar-pyin-gi-mdo;* Skt., *Prajnaparamita-sutra.* This probably refers to the version in eight thousand lines; there are in fact forty-two sutras in this category, the three most important being those of 100,000, 25,000 and 8,000 lines. The last of the three is the most frequently quoted. All three of these "wisdom" sutras, as well as most of the others in the set of forty-two, were translated into English by the late Edward Conze: see *The Large Sutra on Perfect Wisdom* (Berkeley: University of California Press, 1975), *The Short Prajnaparamita Texts* (London: Luzac, 1973), and others.

41. The "etc." here refers to other types of meditation on the transformative nature of being, such as subtle impermanence, non-self-nature, and so forth.

42. The Vajrasattva meditation is explained in detail in *Mahayana Purification,* translated and edited by Brian Beresford (Dharamsala: Library of Tibetan Works and Archives, 1980).

43. *The Sutra Requested by Subahu;* Tib., *dPung-bzang-gis-zhus-bai-mdo;* Skt., *Subahu-pariprccha-tantra.*

44. *The Four Hundred Verses;* Tib., *bZhi-brgya-pa;* Skt., *Catuhshataka-shastra.*

45. *Compendium of Bodhisattva Trainings;* Tib., *bsLab-pa-kun-btus;* Skt., *Shiksha-samucchaya.*

46. *The Sutra of Unfading Wisdom;* Tib., *bLo-gros-mi-zad-pai-mdo;* Skt., *Arya-aksayamati-nirdesha.*

47. *Sutra of the Sacred Mountain;* Tib., *gYak-rii-mdo.* I could not trace this in the *Kangyur* catalogue.

48. *A Guide to the Middle View;* Tib., *dBu-ma-la-'jug-pa;* Skt., *Madhyamaka-avatara.*

49. That is, the fourth of the *brahmaviharas.*

50. *A Letter to a Disciple;* Tib., *sLob-sbring;* Skt., *Shisyalekha.*

51. *Verses Tuned to the Naga King's Drum;* Tib., *kLui-gyal-po-rnga-sgrai-tshigs-bcad;* Skt., *Arya-sagaranagaraja.*

52. *A Precious Garland;* Tib., *Rin-chen-phreng-ba;* Skt., *Ratnavali.*

53. *The Ornament of Clear Realizations;* Tib., *dNgon-rtogs-rgyan;* Skt., *Abhisamaya-alamkara.*

54. *The Stages of Meditation;* Tib., *sGom-rim;* Skt., *Bhavana-krama.*

55. His story is told in the Jataka collection *sKyes-rab-brgya-bcu-pa,* by 'Jam-dbyangs-blo-gter-dbang-po, published in Tibetan by the Library of Tibetan Works and Archives (Dharamsala: 1980). There are hundreds of Buddhist *Jataka* tales, or stories from the Buddha's previous lives. Each one shows how he learned a specific spiritual lesson at a particular stage of the path.

56. This verse is from Shantideva's *Bodhicharyavatara.*

57. *The Sutra Requested by Subahu;* Tib., *dPung-bzang-gis-zhus-bai-mdo;* Skt., *Subahu-pariprccha-tantra.*

58. Tib., dBu-ma-lta-'khrid.

59. Tib., bar-do; the state between death and rebirth.

60. The four opponent forces. These are explained in the section "Purifying the Mind of Negative Karma."

61. A *dzo* is a large animal that is a cross between an ox and a female yak, or *dri.* The idea is simply that we should not burden others with a load that we ourselves are not willing to carry.

Selected Bibliography

Batchelor, Stephen. *The Tibet Guide*. London: Wisdom Publications, 1987.

The Blue Annals. Translated by George Roerich. Calcutta: The Royal Asiatic Society, 1949.

Bridging the Sutras and Tantras: Selected Works of the Dalai Lama I. Compiled, edited and translated by Glenn H. Mullin. Ithaca, New York: Snow Lion Publications, 1981.

Essence of Refined Gold: Selected Works of the Dalai Lama III. Compiled, edited and translated by Glenn H. Mullin. Ithaca, New York: Snow Lion Publications, 1982.

Gyatso, Geshe Kelsang. *Universal Compassion*. London: Tharpa Publications, 1988.

Mahayana Purification. Translated and edited by Brian Beresford. Dharamsala: Library of Tibetan Works and Archives, 1980.

Nagarjuna's Letter: Nagarjuna's 'Letter to a Friend' with a Commentary by the Venerable Rendawa, Zhon-nu Lo-dro. Translated by Geshe Lobsang Tharchin and Artemus B. Engle. Dharamsala: Library of Tibetan Works and Archives, 1979.

Path of the Bodhisattva Warrior: The Life and Teachings of the Thirteenth Dalai Lama. Translated by Glenn H. Mullin. Ithaca, New York: Snow Lion Publications, 1988.

Rabten, Geshe and Geshe Ngawang Dhargyey. *Advice from a Spir-*

itual Friend. Translated by Gonzar Tulku and Brian Beresford. New Delhi: Wisdom Publications, 1977.

Shantideva. *A Guide to the Bodhisattva's Way of Life.* Translated by Stephen Batchelor. Dharamsala: Library of Tibetan Works and Archives, 1981.

Songs of Spiritual Change: Selected Works of the Dalai Lama VII. Compiled, edited and translated by Glenn H. Mullin. Ithaca, New York: Snow Lion Publications, 1982.

The Tibetan Dhammapada. Translated by Gareth Sparham. New Delhi: Mahayana Publications, 1983.

Wallace, B. Alan. *A Passage from Solitude: Training the Mind in a Life Embracing the World.* Edited by Zara Houshmand. Ithaca, New York: Snow Lion Publications, 1992.